How to Conduct a Workplace Human Rights Investigation

A CLV Special Report

Malcolm J. MacKillop, Jamie Knight, Kristin Taylor,

Fraser Milner Casgrain LLP

THOMSON

™

CARSWELL

National Library of Canada Cataloguing in Publication

MacKillop, Malcolm
    How to conduct a workplace human rights
investigation / Malcolm J. MacKillop, Jamie Knight,
Kristin Taylor.

(CLV special report)
ISBN 0-459-28301-4

    1. Sexual harassment--Investigation. I. Knight, Jamie
II. Taylor, Kristin III. Title. IV. Series: CLV special
report series.

HF5549.5.S45M33 2003   658.3'145   C2003-906301-1

THOMSON

CARSWELL

One Corporate Plaza	Customer Relations
2075 Kennedy Road	Toronto 1-416-609-3800
Toronto, Ontario	Elsewhere in Canada/U.S. 1-800-387-5164
M1T 3V4	Fax 1-416-298-5094
	World Wide Web: http://www.carswell.com
	E-mail: orders@carswell.com

About the Authors

Malcolm MacKillop is a senior partner at the Toronto office of Fraser Milner Casgrain LLP. His practice is concentrated on wrongful dismissal, human rights, and litigating including providing strategic advice to employers on all employment related matters. Malcolm is listed as a leading practitioner in Employment Law in Lexpert. He provides advice in both the private and public sectors and has appeared as an expert in human rights on numerous TV and radio shows including Pamela Wallin, The Fifth Estate, W5, CBC – The National, CBC – The Journal and Global Television.

Jamie Knight is the Manager of the Employment/Pension/Research Department in the Toronto office of Fraser Milner Casgrain LLP. Jamie received his law degree from the University of Toronto in 1983 and was called to the Ontario Bar in 1985. Jamie has been an employment and labour lawyer throughout his career. He represents unionized employers in collective agreement negotiations, at arbitrations and before the Ontario Labour Relations Board and various other administrative tribunals in the labour and employment law field, including the public sector.

Kristin Taylor is a partner at the Toronto office of Fraser Milner Casgrain LLP. She provides practical and strategic advice to employers on a wide range of employment matters, including employee hiring; discipline and termination; severance packages; corporate restructuring; employment agreements and personnel policies; certification applications; privacy compliancy; and employment standards and human rights issues.

Dedication

To my beautiful son, Evan Batten-Cotte, who inspires me to appreciate the "small stuff" in life and to be thankful for all my worldly gifts …

Malcolm MacKillop

To my late grandmother, Dorothy Glen Tucker, who was the first Female Trustee ever elected to the Protestant School Board of Greater Montreal, in the 1950's. My grandmother went by her middle name all of her adult life. When she arrived at her first Board meeting, all of her fellow trustees assumed that my grandmother was a secretary and wondered when the new man, Glen, would arrive. Nobody had to ask who Glen was by the second meeting.

Jamie Knight

To my daughter, Beth, for making what Mom does matter and my husband, John, for his love of instruction manuals.

Kristin Taylor

Acknowledgments

This book would not have been possible without the dedicated work of our colleague Nadine Cote. Nadine spent many hours coordinating earlier work that each of us had done, developing the text, checking cases and referencing statutes. Nadine is in her fifth year of practice. She is a senior associate in our employment and labour group. In addition to acting as an advisor and advocate for employers and senior employees, Nadine has been a contributor to the CCH publication, Canadian Employment & Equality Rights, specializing in recent developments in human rights law, and has made a number of presentations to HRPAO district organizations. We are very grateful to Nadine for her contributions.

♦
PREFACE

Conducting a workplace investigation is stressful, time-consuming and if improperly managed, can have serious impacts on your workplace.

Every investigation is important and will generally have some degree of impact on the people involved and on the corporate culture. There are usually many vested interests which must be recognized by the investigators before an investigation even begins. In a harassment investigation, you have the complainant who perceives himself or herself as a victim and the respondent—the person who stands accused of the complaint. Both parties have different pressing concerns which have to be considered and responded to by the company. Both parties, depending on the outcome of the investigation, risk suffering a change in their employment.

For the company, many investigations provide an opportunity for the company to "walk the talk", to show its commitment to providing its employees with a healthy and safe work environment.

Unfortunately, a flawed investigation generally leads to an improper analysis of the issues and to an incorrect conclusion. Conversely, an investigation which is properly conducted can lead to a resolution of the complaint and a minimization of the risks of litigation. A properly conducted investigation can also increase employee morale and the level of commitment that employees feel towards the company.

The purpose of this book is to provide the reader with a sound understanding of the legal principles that inherently come into play in every investigation and to also provide a practical and common sense approach to many of the complicated issues that typically arise during an investigation.

The authors have conducted numerous investigations on their own and have provided clients in many different industries with guidance on how to conduct a proper investigation. Although every investigation is unique and there can never be just one way to proceed, there are recurring issues that surface in every investigation which this book has attempted to address.

As a word of caution, although we collectively feel that our approach on most of the issues canvassed in this book seem to work the best, it is always important for you to proceed in a way that you are the most comfortable with and which properly responds to the unique facts that you are faced with.

Malcolm MacKillop
Jamie Knight
Kristin Taylor

◆
FOREWORD

Harassment is one form of discrimination. Canadian law has made remarkable progress in dealing with harassment in our society, institutions and workplaces, but the task is incomplete. The issue of harassment continues to exist and will not be eradicated any time soon.

Human rights law is one of the instruments by which we seek to curb and redress harassment and promote the objective of allowing each citizen, regardless of sex, race or other characteristics, to realize his or her full potential.

Human rights law aims to support inclusion and respect for all in society, to recognize the dignity of every person, to promote equal rights and opportunities free of discrimination and harassment, and the promotion of full participation by all.

Harassment in the workplace is illegal and wrong. Most employers and employees know that discrimination is illegal and wrong, yet the issue of harassment continues to be rife in workplaces. This issue continues to abound because some employers and employees do not understand or simply refuse to accept human rights laws that prohibit harassment in the workplace.

This book is an invaluable resource to all employers and employees. It explains your legal obligation to protect and advance the rights of every person in the workplace. It also tells you how to deal effectively and expediently with issues of discrimination and harassment in the workplace.

This book provides straightforward explanations and practical suggestions to prevent harassment and to deal with it effectively if it surfaces in your workplace.

It is imperative for all Canadians to continue to be vigilant in the quest to eradicate all forms of discrimination in Canadian society, institutional systems, and workplaces. It is vital that we commit and continue to address and find creative instruments and mechanisms to resolve and redress the issue of discrimination.

Neil P. Edwards,
Director, Mediation and Investigation
Ontario Human Rights Commission

◆
INTRODUCTION

Harassment was a serious workplace issue as the twentieth century drew to a close and remains so in the early part of this new century. Recent events, whether local or international, frequently make modern life seem like a harsh and angry existence, full of misunderstanding and a lack of respect for other people. The protection of individual rights has been a centrepiece of modern societies, especially since the worst excesses of the Second World War. Human rights law seeks to provide standards of right conduct between individuals and in the context of typical human activity, such as where people live, where they play, and where they work.

Protection against unwarranted discrimination and harassment are the centrepieces of human rights law. You could say that harassment is simply a particular kind of discrimination; however, as we will soon see, harassment has its own identifying features and requires a particular kind of response that typically focuses on individual misconduct.

The focus of this book is on the prevention of harassment in Canadian workplaces and how incidents of harassment should be investigated by employers. We take it for granted that all reasonable employers will oppose harassment as a general matter of principle. That may not be enough, no matter how benevolent the employer, how well drafted its human rights policies or how attentive it is to appropriate procedures and practices. In addition to a general statement of principle and attention to preventing harassment in general, there are two very good reasons for employers to be concerned about individual situations of harassment.

The first reason is that harassment in the workplace is against the law. Although worded somewhat differently in each jurisdiction, this general proposition applies throughout Canada.[1] Employers have a positive legal duty to protect employees from harassment. It is certainly important for

---

[1]   As with all employment law in Canada, human rights law, including harassment, falls within provincial jurisdiction for the most part and each province has human rights legislation. The *Canadian Human Rights Act*, R.S.C. 1985, c. H-6, as amended, applies to federal workplaces.

employers to have proper policies in place, which will promote workplaces that are harmonious, tolerant, and respectful. As well, employers must be conscientious in implementing those policies. More than this, employers have a specific duty to take action when they discover specific incidents of harassment. Employers must be alert to the potential for harassment; wilful blindness is not acceptable. When discovered, harassment has to be pulled up by the roots and steps have to be taken to try to prevent its recurrence, whether with this aggressor or other potential bullies.

The second reason is that to prevent harassment is ethical and good for business. In a workplace that allows harassment to fester and breed, employees may experience stress, increased absenteeism, low productivity, low morale and strained relations at work and at home. Harassment rarely goes away on its own; in fact, it often gets worse and harder to address with time. In addition to reduced productivity, increased employee turnover, and harm to reputation, employers who fail to take effective measures to combat harassment may face costly legal proceedings, including liability for the damages suffered by affected employees.

Employees have developed a heightened awareness of their right to work in a harassment-free environment, and are increasingly taking action against not only the aggressors, but also the employers who fail to protect their rights.

So what precisely is harassment? What are the legal obligations of employers to prevent harassment in the workplace? What should employers do when they receive a complaint of workplace harassment? How should an investigation be conducted? What happens after the investigation has been completed? How can employers limit their liability and reduce legal costs? Practical answers to these questions and more will be found in the pages that follow. Our objective is to provide you with straightforward explanations and practical suggestions to prevent harassment and to deal with it if it shows up in your workplace.

Brief Contents

Contents

♦

CHAPTER 1

HARASSMENT IN THE WORKPLACE

1. Harassment Defined

At root, harassment is a pattern of offensive behaviour, directed by an aggressor against a victim or group, motivated by such prohibited grounds as the gender, sexual orientation, age, disabling condition, race or religious beliefs of the victim. As we will see, the concept of harassment has evolved, but this root definition is a good starting point. The behaviour in question, whether words or deeds, is generally known by the aggressor to be unwelcome. In other words, in most situations, the bully intends the victim to be offended by the conduct in question. At the very least, the aggressor ought to know that the conduct is unwelcome. That is, a reasonable person would understand that engaging in this kind of speech or conduct would be offensive to the individual target of the activity. The unwelcome conduct is typically repeated over a period of time and there may well be multiple victims. The conduct is usually verbal or physical in nature, but it may be expressed in subtle forms, such as shunning, the way one person looks at another, or comments made about others behind their backs.

Harassment has been more precisely defined as engaging in a course of vexatious comment or conduct that demeans, humiliates or embarrasses a person and is known or ought reasonably to be known to be unwelcome.[1] Other concepts that will emerge in the pages that follow include the poisoned workplace, special forms of sexual harassment that occur between supervisors and subordinates, and the employer's liability for workplace harassment even when the employer neither knows nor approves of the impugned conduct, and whether or not it occurs in the physical workplace.

1.a. Preventing Personal Harassment in the Workplace

Employers have a positive responsibility to foster workplaces free from harassment, and to react promptly and effectively when incidents of harassment arise. We will take a closer look at the legal nature of this responsibility in the following chapter. In addition to the responsibility of employers, it is important to understand that most cases of workplace harassment are personal, by one employee to another. The offence of harassment overlaps with and is closely linked to the criminal offence of assault. It is conduct that our society considers to be intolerable, by one person, visited upon another. Employers play a very important role in our modern society. We have high expectations of our employers. In respect of personal harassment, we expect that our employers will take a leading role in preventing it, finding it, and stamping it out.

1.b. Single Incident

Harassment generally involves a pattern of behaviour over a period of time. Persistent and repeated behaviour is usually required to create the abusive environment consistent with harassment. However, there are exceptions where a single incident is so serious that it constitutes harassment in breach of human rights legislation.[2] The severity of the conduct determines whether repetition is necessary to meet the harassment test. A physical assault, for example, need not be repeated in order to amount to

---

[1] Ontario *Human Rights Code*, R.S.O. 1990, c. H.19, as amended, s. 10(1).

[2] Ontario Human Rights Commission, *Policy on Sexual Harassment and Inappropriate Gender-Related Comments and Conduct*, (1996) at 5-9, online: Ontario Human Rights Commission, <http:// www.ohrc.on.ca/English/publications/sexual-harassment-policy.pdf> (date accessed: 26 September 2003).

sexual harassment.[3] Also, if adverse employment consequences follow from the rejection of an unwanted sexual advance, repetition may not be required. More subtle conduct, such as off-colour jokes and remarks, will usually require a pattern to amount to harassment.

1.c.   Limited Relevance of Intent

By definition, it is not necessary that a person actually turn his or her mind to the question of whether or not the impugned activity is offensive to the "target" employee. It is sufficient if that employee is offended and if it should have been clear to the aggressor that the conduct would be taken as unwelcome. In other words, all that is required to find harassment is to establish that a person intended to engage in the actions that form the basis for the complaint. You do not have to establish that the aggressor actually considered the impact that these actions would have on the person or persons to whom they were directed.

1.d.   Poisoned Work Environment

Harassment can create what is referred to as a "poisoned work environment", which is a negative and offensive workplace environment. Employees can rightfully complain about harassment caused by the existence of a poisoned work environment, even if they are not the subject of the harassment. For example, a woman could overhear a male manager telling another male that women are not good managers. Although the comment was not directed at the woman who overheard it, she may feel uncomfortable at work because of it, and discouraged from applying for management positions. The comment, in isolation, may not amount to much, but it could become much more significant if linked with other such comments or inappropriate conduct that routinely occurs in the workplace. These types of comments, even if not directed at someone, can accumulate to create a poisoned work environment.

Poisoned work environments can also be created through hearsay or the spreading of rumours as opposed to direct experience. For example, an employee may be informed by a co-worker that other employees refer to him behind his back by racial slurs. The co-worker may be well-intentioned or devious. The information may be accurate or distorted.

---

[3]   See *Re Canada Post Corp. and Canadian Union of Postal Workers* (1983), 11 L.A.C. (3d) 13 (Norman) in which a supervisor put his hands on a female subordinate's hips and pressed his body against her buttocks. This brief, single incident was found to be sexual harassment.

However solid the basis, the spreading of the word can create a poisoned work environment if the result of the disclosure causes the employee to feel that the working environment is uncomfortable, unwelcome or even intolerable.[4]

Where repeated comments or, in the case of sexual harassment, sexual encounters, create a poisoned work environment, there is no need for a complainant to prove an adverse employment-related decision. The existence of the poisoned work environment is, on its own, sufficient to establish harassment.

1.e. Examples of Harassment

Examples of harassment in employment include the following:

- Derogatory remarks about a person's religious beliefs;
- Jokes about a person's place of origin or name-calling;
- The display of racist or offensive images, including posters and computer screensavers; and
- Unwelcome invitations or requests of a sexual nature.

2. Sexual Harassment Defined

In the majority of workplaces, harassment that is gender-based is most likely to generate complaints. The most common types of gender harassment involve sexual actions, comments or requests for sexual "favours" that are made in the course of employment. This kind of activity constitutes sexual harassment if the harasser knows or ought reasonably to know that his or her conduct is unwelcome. A universal definition of sexual harassment has not been adopted by Canadian adjudicators; however, the Supreme Court of Canada's broad definition from well over a decade ago is useful: "unwelcome conduct of a sexual nature that detrimentally affects the work environment or leads to adverse job-related consequences for the victims of the harassment".[5]

Sexual harassment includes sexual solicitations and reprisals. These particular forms of harassment involve a person who is in a position of authority using his or her power to pressure a subordinate employee into engaging in sexual activities, or to exact a measure of revenge in the case

---

[4]   See *Pillai v. Lafarge Canada Inc.* (June 13, 2003), T Beharrell Member, [2003] B.C.H.R.T.D. No. 26 (B.C. Human Rights Trib.).

[5]   *Janzen v. Platy Enterprises Ltd.*, [1989] 1 S.C.R. 1252 (S.C.C.) at 1284.

of an aggressor who is rebuffed. These kinds of situations arise if decisions affecting a person's employment are based on submission to or rejection of sexual advances, or if a supervisor makes threats to that effect.

2.a. Gender-Based Harassment

We purposefully used the phrase "gender-based" harassment to make the point that sexual harassment may not be based on sexual activity. Harassment based on gender may include harassing comments or conduct because of stereotypical features of one gender or the other, or that are directed to an identifiable group whose common feature is gender. For example, a manager may constantly interrupt a woman during meetings, but not the men; a man may make derogatory comments to women in the workplace who take maternity leave; or a woman may target a man for abuse based on characteristically male features or behaviour. The expression or implication of sexual unattractiveness through demeaning comments of a sexual nature will constitute sexual harassment where it is repetitive and has the effect of creating an offensive working environment.[6]

Most sexual harassment complaints are filed by women against men. However, men file complaints against women, and harassment by individuals of the same sex is also against the law irrespective of the individuals' sexual orientation. Gender-based harassment includes harassment based on sexual orientation. As with typical sexual harassment, sexual orientation harassment can be sexual in nature or not sexual at all, but based on conduct or remarks that are directed towards people because of their sexual orientation.

2.b. Consent

There is an endless variety of personal relationships. What may appear on the surface to involve an imbalance of power actually may be entirely respectful and consensual with no improper motives or conduct, at least in terms of the impact on the workplace, other employees, or third parties. Even so, when a person in a supervisory or management role is in an intimate relationship with a subordinate employee, especially if that relationship is kept hidden, it is at least dangerous, probably contrary to the interests of the employer, and possibly a situation of harassment in the context of sexual solicitation and reprisals. The greater the power imbalance, the

---

[6] See *Shaw v. Levac Supply Ltd.* (1990), 91 C.L.L.C. 17,007 (Ont. Bd. of Inquiry) at 16, 181.

greater the risk to the manager and the employer. There are relationships that are so dramatically imbalanced that consent is impossible to ascertain. A relationship between the President of the United States and an intern is the most obvious example of such a power imbalance, with popular perception being that consent was irrelevant to the impropriety of the President's conduct.

Moreover, such relationships are not static, nor are the surrounding circumstances. A relationship may start off as consensual, but if the subordinate begins to reconsider, it becomes very difficult to determine which advances were welcome and which were not. Working relationships that have involved what appeared to be consensual sexual relations, at least at a certain point in time, have resulted in findings of sexual harassment.[7] Human rights tribunals have found that voluntarily sexual intercourse can amount to sexual harassment where the complainant is vulnerable due to the supervisory relationship—even if there are no threats of reprisal for saying no.[8] It may not be necessary for a subordinate employee to voice actual protest. The manager ultimately bears the burden of proving that the subordinate welcomed the sexual conduct and continued to welcome it at all stages in the relationship.

2.c.   Intimate Relationships in the Workplace

Two cases illustrate the difficulty of determining whether an intimate relationship between an employee and a manager is consensual or unwelcome. In *Dupuis v. British Columbia (Ministry of Forests)*, the complainant was a graduate student hired by a professor as a research coordinator. They had sexual intercourse at the outset of their working relationship on multiple occasions. The complainant did not allege that the sexual conduct was coerced through physical force or threats of adverse consequences if she did

---

[7]   See *Mahmoodi v. Dutton* (1999)*University of British Columbia*, [1999] B.C.H.R.T.D. No. 52, 1999 CarswellBC 3088 (B.C. Human Rights Trib.), affirmed (2001), 95 B.C.L.R. (3d) 186 (B.C. S.C. QL,) [hereinafter *Mahmoodi v. University of British* Columbia]; application for judicial review dismissed at *Dutton v. British Columbia (Human Rights Tribunal)*, [2001] B.C.. *Radloff v. Stox Broadcast Corp.* (1999), [1999] B.C.H.R.T.D. No. 36, 1999 CarswellBC 3173 (B.C. Human Rights Trib.); *Dupuis v. British Columbia (Ministry of Forest)* (1993), [1993] B.C.C.H.R.D. No. 43, 20 C.H.R.R. D/87 (B.C. Human Rights Council) [hereinafter *Dupois v. British Columbia (Ministry of Forests)*], *Vanderwell Contractors (1971) Ltd. v. C. (J.)* (2001), 40 C.H.R.R. D/505 (Alta. Human Rights Bd. of Inquiry), affirmed (2001), 44 C.H.R.R. D/266 (Alta. Q.B.), online: Alberta Human Rights Commission <http://www . albertahumanrights . ab . ca/legislation/Panel_Decisions/panel.decisChartrand.asp> (date accessed: 29 September 2003).

[8]   *Dupuis v. British Columbia (Ministry of Forests)*, *supra*, note 7 at para. 47.

not acquiesce. She maintained, however, that although she didn't say "no" or voice opposition to the sexual relationship that developed, it was not welcome. The British Columbia Council of Human Rights noted that it would have been preferable for the complainant to have been more explicit in her feelings. However, it went on to find that despite the professor's genuine belief that his sexual advances were welcome, he should have known they were not. According to this tribunal, "voluntariness is merely a fact to consider in considering whether the conduct was welcome."[9] The employer was held liable for over $20,000 in damages to the complainant on account of the professor's sexual harassment.

An equally complicated scenario presented itself in *Radloff v. Stox Broadcast Corp.*[10] Ms. Radloff had an "intimate personal relationship" with Mr. Schroeder that ended before he hired her as a receptionist at the company of which he was president. During her employment, Ms. Radloff was promoted but also subjected to unwelcome comments from Mr. Schroeder and, in one case, a consultant to the company. After Mr. Schroeder attempted to rekindle the relationship and delivered a formal marriage proposal to Ms. Radloff, she subsequently left the workplace and filed a sexual harassment complaint. Her complaint succeeded and, although Mr. Schroeder argued that his employer should not be liable for his conduct, the tribunal disagreed. Mr. Schroeder's employer was found liable for his sexual harassment.

What may seem to be nobody else's business may become something quite different if the supervisor ends up determining whom to lay-off or promote, when the subordinate employee is one of the candidates. As well, the consensual nature of the relationship may come under attack when the relationship ends, particularly if the subordinate employee ends up without a job. It is very hard to impose rules on adults who feel that they are involved in a private situation that they feel is characterized by trust and even love. If these adults are in the same workplace and there is a power imbalance between them, especially if they work in close proximity, they have to understand that, from a human rights standpoint, especially in terms of harassment, their relationship is fraught with risk.

---

[9]   *Ibid*, at para. 50.
[10]   *Supra*, note 5.

7

2.d.   Examples of Sexual Harassment

Examples of harassment in employment based on gender, sex or sexual orientation include the following:

- Degrading remarks about either sex;
- Unwelcome touching;
- Unwelcome sexual requests, remarks, jokes or gestures;
- Displaying sexually offensive pictures;
- Sending sexually offensive e-mail communications;
- Leering or inappropriate staring; and
- Unfair evaluations or reprimands, changes to terms and conditions of work, or dismissal from employment when they are in retaliation to objecting to sexual harassment.

3. Harassment Under Human Rights Legislation - Prohibited Grounds

As we have noted, all provinces, the territories and the federal jurisdiction have human rights legislation in force. Human rights legislation in every Canadian jurisdiction prohibits harassment in employment based on the following grounds (often simply referred to as the "prohibited grounds" or the "protected grounds"):

- race, colour, ancestry, citizenship, place of origin, ethnic origin and/or national origin;
- creed or religion;
- age, although the definition of age varies by jurisdiction;
- marital status;
- family status;
- disability, whether physical or mental;
- sex, which includes pregnancy; and
- sexual orientation, which includes homosexuality, heterosexuality and bisexuality.

Certain jurisdictions prohibit harassment in employment based on additional grounds. Harassment based on receipt of public assistance or social condition is prohibited in Alberta[11], Manitoba[12], Newfoundland and Labra-

---

[11]   *Human Rights, Citizenship and Multiculturalism Act*, R.S.A. 2000, c. H-14, s. 7(1).
[12]   *Human Rights Code*, C.C.S.M. c. H175, s. 9.

dor[13], Nova Scotia[14], the Northwest Territories[15], Prince Edward Island[16], Quebec[17], Saskatchewan[18] and is expected to be prohibited in Nunavut,[19] when its human rights legislation is passed. Political beliefs, opinion and/or association is a protected ground in British Columbia[20], Manitoba[21], Newfoundland and Labrador[22], the Northwest Territories[23], Prince Edward Island[24], Quebec[25], and the Yukon[26]. Discrimination based on a criminal or summary conviction offence that is unrelated to employment is a ground upon which harassment in employment is prohibited in British Columbia[27], Prince Edward Island[28] and Quebec[29]. Ontario[30] prohibits discrimination based on record of offences and the federal jurisdiction[31] prohibits discrimination based on a pardoned conviction.

As of June 1, 2004, the concept of prohibited harassment will be very broadly expanded within the province of Quebec. Legislation has passed prohibiting "psychological harassment" in Quebec workplaces. Psychological harassment is defined expansively as "any vexatious behaviour in the form of repeated and hostile or unwanted conduct, verbal comments, actions or gestures, that affects an employee's dignity or psychological or physical integrity and that results in a harmful work environment for the employee".[32] By statute, employers are obliged to take reasonable steps to prevent psychological harassment and, whenever they become aware of it, to put a stop to it. These provisions will be deemed to be a part of every collective agreement in the province of Quebec so that harassment complaints can form the subject of a unionized employee's grievance. Non-

---

[13] *Human Rights Code*, R.S.N.L. 1990, c. H-14, s. 9.
[14] *Human Rights Act*, R.S.N.S. 1989, c. 214, s. 5.
[15] *Human Rights Act*, S.N.W.T. 2002, c.18, s. 5 *note: this statute is awaiting royal proclamation.
[16] *Human Rights Act*, R.S.P.E.I. 1988, c. H-12, ss. 1 and 6.
[17] *Charter of Human Rights and Freedoms*, R.S.Q., c. C-12, ss. 10 and 18.2.
[18] *Saskatchewan Human Rights Code*, S.S. 1979, c. S-24.1, s. 2 and 16.
[19] Bill 12, *Human Rights Act* 6th Sess., 1st Leg., Nunavut, 2002, s. 7 (2nd reading 31 October 2002).
[20] *Human Rights Code*, R.S.B.C. 1996, c. 210, s. 13.
[21] *Supra,* note 13.
[22] *Supra,* note 14.
[23] *Supra,* note 16.
[24] *Supra,* note 17.
[25] *Supra,* note 18.
[26] *Human Rights Act,* R.S.Y. 2002, c. 116, s. 7.
[27] *Supra,* note 21.
[28] *Supra,* note 17.
[29] *Supra,* note 18.
[30] *Supra,* note 2 at ss. 5 and 7.
[31] *Supra,* note 1 at ss. 3 and 14.
[32] *An Act Respecting Labour Standards*, R.S.Q., c. N-1.1, c. 45, s. 81.18.

unionized employees will be able to complain to the Commission Des Norms Du Travail.

Some jurisdictions distinguish between the grounds of prohibited discrimination and grounds of prohibited harassment; however, most jurisdictions only state the grounds of prohibited discrimination. This is a difference without consequence because it is readily accepted, whenever necessary for the purposes of statutory interpretation and application, that harassment is a form of discrimination.[33]

As noted above, these grounds of harassment are usually collectively referred to as the "prohibited grounds" of harassment. Human rights legislation does not prohibit harassment in general; rather, the harassment must be based on one or more of the specific prohibited grounds. For example, an employee who claims that he was harassed at work by another employee for chewing gum would have no basis to complain under human rights legislation, without being able to link chewing gum to a prohibited ground of harassment.

4. Personal Harassment

Employees often complain about harassment from a supervisor, either in the imposition of discipline, management of attendance, or simply day-to-day supervision. Even if there is a legitimate question about the appropriateness of the supervisor's conduct, this claim of "harassment" does not fall with the purview of human rights law unless it can properly fit within a prohibited ground, such as gender or race. Harassment that is alleged to have occurred for reasons other than a prohibited ground is best characterized as "personal harassment". Personal harassment typically involves unwelcome and offensive conduct or an abuse of authority. It is important to emphasize that a personality conflict with a supervisor or proper performance management by a supervisor do not constitute personal harassment. Arbitrators who have considered union grievances alleging personal harassment have established a test that management's direction must be demeaning and vexatious, designed primarily to embarrass and annoy rather than achieve a legitimate business purpose to constitute personal harassment.[34]

---

[33] *Supra,* note 6.

[34] *Toronto (City) v. C.U.P.E., Local 43* (1991), 19 L.A.C. (4th) 412 (Ont. Arb. Bd.) (Davis) and *Clearbrook Grain & Milling Co. v. U.F.C.W., Local 1518* (2000), 93 L.A.C. (4th) 312 (Can. Arb. Bd.) (Burke).

Personal harassment can constitute just cause for discipline and, in severe cases, the termination of an employee's employment.[35] It is just as unacceptable in the workplace as harassment on prohibited grounds and should be similarly stamped out. That being said, how an employer reacts to allegations of personal harassment may be different in that a full-blown investigation may not be required and less formal means may be employed as outlined in Chapter 4 below.

5. Protection against Reprisals

Protection is provided to those who seek to enforce their rights under human rights legislation. Human rights legislation prohibits reprisals and threats of reprisals against individuals who make claims and who seek to enforce their human rights. Reprisals can come in various forms, such as a demotion, the denial of a promotion or wage increase, an unwanted transfer, or dismissal from employment. A reprisal complaint can succeed in the absence of a successful complaint alleging discrimination.

We note that this kind of protection against reprisals is common to most employment legislation. This should not be confused with, and is in addition to, the protection against reprisals that is specific to sexual solicitations. In other words, there is a special kind of reprisal protection to protect subordinate employees from threats or negative employment consequences, such as lay-offs or lost promotion or overtime opportunities, related to improper and unwelcome sexual advances from a supervisor.

6. Remedies

Victims of harassment in the workplace have a number of options to consider in seeking redress. Employees may file a formal complaint of harassment under the applicable human rights legislation. The Supreme Court of Canada has determined that employees cannot sue their employers for discrimination or harassment that is prohibited by human rights legislation.[36] Instead, employees who claim harassment are compelled to use the human rights regimes established by legislation. Harassment is not a stand-

---

[35] *University of Victoria and C.U.P.E.* (1995), [1995] B.C.C.A.A.A. No. 520 Award no. X-76/95 (Chertkow), online: QL (ARB) and *Re Brooks Health Centre and H.S.A.A.* (May 24, 1995), 39 C.L.A.S. 396, 095/199/076 (Tettensor, Mearns, Currie).

[36] *Bhadauria v. Seneca College of Applied Arts & Technology*, [1981] 2 S.C.R. 181 (S.C.C.).

alone cause of action under common law. That being said, employees still may make allegations of harassment in a number of forums.

6.a.   Unionized Employees

In unionized workplaces, employees' terms and conditions of work are contained in the collective agreement negotiated between the union and the employer. Often collective agreements contain provisions that protect employees from harassment on the prohibited grounds. Some collective agreements exceed the prohibited grounds and prohibit harassment in any form. In these instances, employers will be obligated to prevent all forms of harassment and to investigate all allegations of harassment, even if not otherwise required to do so under human rights legislation. If the right to freedom from harassment is set out in the collective agreement, a unionized employee can pursue a violation of this right through the grievance and arbitration procedure that is a necessary feature of every collective agreement. Even if there is no right to freedom from harassment in the collective agreement or if the collective agreement prohibits an employee, such as a probationary employee, from accessing the grievance procedure, labour law in some jurisdictions notionally incorporates the substantive rights and obligations of human rights legislation into the collective agreement. In either case, whether or not the right to freedom from harassment is spelled out, arbitrators are empowered to enforce such a right.[37]

Unionized employees generally are precluded from suing their employers where the dispute, in its essential character, arises from the interpretation, application, administration or violation of the collective agreement.[38] In some Canadian jurisdictions, they also may be precluded from filing complaints of harassment with human rights commissions.[39] Human rights commissions generally are required to evaluate on a case-by-case basis whether a complaint could more appropriately be dealt with under the grievance procedure provided by the collective agreement applicable to the complainant.[40] An arbitrator, therefore, may be the ultimate decision-maker in harassment cases involving unionized employees.

---

[37]   *Parry Sound (District) Welfare Administration Board v. O.P.S.E.U., Local 324* (2003), [2003] S.C.J. No. 42, 2003 CarswellOnt 3500 (S.C.C.).

[38]   *Weber v. Ontario Hydro*, [1995] 2 S.C.R. 929 (S.C.C.).

[39]   See *Chapman v. 3M Canada Inc.* (1997), 30 C.C.E.L. (2d) 102 (Ont. C.A.).

[40]   See *Thomas v. Ontario (Human Rights Commission)* (2001), 12 C.C.E.L. (3d) 14 (Ont. C.A.) and *Snaggers v. Alberta (Human Rights Commission)* (2000), 193 D.L.R. (4th) 120 (Alta. C.A.), leave to appeal refused (2001), 274 N.R. 198 (note) (S.C.C.).

An arbitration hearing is conducted in a more informal fashion than a court proceeding, although many of the same rules apply. At an arbitration hearing, the union representative and the employer representative make opening statements, call witnesses to testify, cross-examine each other's witnesses and make closing arguments that draw conclusions from the evidence presented and apply the law. The arbitrator appointed to hear the case, whether on agreement by the parties or through a government-mandated system, renders a decision that is final and binding on the parties. Arbitrators have broad powers including compensation for lost wages and benefits and reinstatement.

6.b.   Complaints to Human Rights Commissions

Whether or not an employer has an internal complaint process and has conducted an investigation, and subject to special rules for unionized employees, an employee may file a complaint of harassment contrary to a protected ground with the applicable human rights commission. As you would expect, an employee is far more likely to file a formal human rights complaint if there is no internal process or if the employee is dissatisfied with the employer's handling of the complaint.

Except in British Columbia, when a human rights commission receives a complaint, its initial role is twofold.[41] In no particular order, the two roles initially played by a human rights commission are mediation/conciliation and investigation. If the matter is not settled through mediation or conciliation, after the investigation is concluded, the complaint will either be closed or referred to a tribunal for hearing. At a tribunal hearing, the human rights commission no longer plays the role of the neutral investigator or settlement facilitator. Once the subject matter of a complaint has been referred to a tribunal for hearing, the human rights commission becomes the advocate for the complainant. The complainant may also have independent counsel. The hearing proceeds in similar fashion to the grievance arbitration hearing described above.

The powers of human rights tribunals in respect of granting remedies are defined by statute and vary somewhat by jurisdiction. What is universal, however, is the broad remedial power to do whatever is necessary, in the opinion of the tribunal, to comply with the legislation in respect of the

---

[41]   It should be noted that British Columbia amended its *Human Rights Code* to eliminate its Human Rights Commission entirely effective March 31, 2003. Human rights complaints in this province now proceed directly to a Human Rights Tribunal without any investigation by a Commission.

particular complaint before it, as well as future practices.[42] This may involve orders such as reinstatement, payment of damages, educational training, the posting of legal requirements on employee bulletin boards or reading-out orders to employees in the workplace, promotions, provision of letters of reference, and relocation of harassers.

Human rights tribunals can and do get creative in seeking to remedy injustices they have found to have occurred. In a racial harassment case, *McKinnon v. Ontario (Ministry of Correctional Services)*, the human rights board of inquiry, among other things, ordered the employer to read out its order at all-employee gatherings each day for five consecutive days, to attach it to the pay slips of its personnel, and to publish it in its employee newsletter.

The ability to reinstate is conferred by statute. It is a powerful remedy in a human rights context, particularly given the lengthy delay that appears to be inherent in the processing of human rights complaints. Although human rights commissions in many Canadian jurisdictions have reduced the length of time required to process complaints, it generally remains years before a complaint is decided at a public hearing.[43] In *Naraine v. Ford Motor Co. of Canada*,[44] a human rights board of inquiry ordered reinstatement in a harassment case where the complainant had been dismissed for assaulting a co-worker, over 11 years later and despite the incident that had led to his dismissal. The reinstatement order, however, was reversed on appeal.

Human rights tribunals also universally have the power to order restitution, including monetary compensation for losses arising out of the harassment, as well as to compensate for mental anguish caused by the harassment. These damages may very well exceed the damages to which an employee would be entitled to under common law in the event of a termination of employment. Compensation for lost wages can extend through to the date of the decision of the tribunal.[45] Awards of general damages, however, are quite limited in Canada. In Ontario, the *Human Rights Code* imposes a maximum award for mental anguish at $10,000.[46] Tribunals in ju-

---

[42] *Supra*, note 2 at s. 41(1)(a).

[43] *Supra*, note 42.

[44] (1996), [1996] O.H.R.B.I.D. No. 43, 28 C.H.R.R. D/267 (Ont. Bd. of Inquiry), affirmed (1999), [1999] O.J. No. 2530, 1999 CarswellOnt 2074 (Ont. Div. Ct.), reversed (2001), 41 C.H.R.R. D/349 (Ont. C.A.), leave to appeal refused (2002), 302 N.R. 395 (note) (S.C.C.).

[45] *Knight v. Vancouver Ticket Centre Ltd.* (1998), [1998] B.C.H.R.T.D. No. 53, 1998 CarswellBC 3182 (B.C. Human Rights Trib.).

[46] *Supra*, note 1 at s. 41(1)(b).

risdictions without a similar cap on general damages for mental anguish and suffering relating to discrimination or harassment tend to follow the Ontario trend even without the same legislative requirement. Human rights tribunals may also order general damages for compensation for violations of the Code. Awards of general damages have ranged from $750 to $10,000.[47] However, in a case involving multiple incidents, the tribunal can award monetary damages for each violation of the Code.

Aside from either an express or notional cap on damages for mental distress, the other restriction on the broad remedial power of human rights tribunals is that they cannot order a harasser to apologize.[48] An apology may be an important remedy for a complainant that is available exclusively through an internal complaint resolution process.

6.c.   Civil Actions

Although workplace harassment is not a stand-alone cause of action under Canadian law, harassment can appear in a civil action in two ways. First, a victim of workplace harassment may feel that the circumstances of the harassment effectively breach his or her contract of employment with the employer. Such a victim may sue his or her employer for constructive dismissal based on the harassment itself, the employer's handling of the complaint and/or how the complaint was resolved. Second, an employee whom an employer has found to have engaged in workplace harassment and dismissed for cause may sue his or her employer for wrongful dismissal.

(a) 6.c.i.   Constructive Dismissal Claims by the Victim

In a constructive dismissal claim, an employee asserts that the employer unilaterally breached a material term of his or her employment contract. In other words, the employee claims to have been effectively fired because of some action or inaction on the part of the employer, even though the employer clearly did not tell the employee that his or her employment had been terminated. Harassment in the workplace has been found to constitute a fundamental breach of an employment contract. As a result, although a

---

[47]   See *McKinnon v. Ontario (Ministry of Correctional Services)* (1998), [1998] O.H.R.B.I.D. No. 10, 1998 CarswellOnt 5895 (Ont. Bd. of Inquiry) at para. 311-316, online: QL (BCHR) and *Naraine v. Ford Motor Co. (O.H.R.B.) supra*, note 45, at para. 43.

[48]   *Stevenson v. Canada (Security Intelligence Service)* (2001), 41 C.H.R.R. D/433 (Can. Human Rights Trib.), reversed (2003), 229 F.T.R 297 (Fed. T.D.).

cause of action cannot be based upon harassment alone, harassment may be very relevant in assessing whether the employer's conduct amounted to constructive dismissal.[49]

6.c.ii.   Wrongful Dismissal Claims Involving the Harasser

The legal standard to dismiss an employee for just cause is generally a difficult one to satisfy. Only the most serious, wilful or intentional misconduct that irrevocably fractures the employment relationship will meet the standard. Although there may have been some debate as to whether engaging in sexual harassment constituted just cause for termination,[50] since 1998 the law has been clear: it does. In companion decisions released the same day, the Ontario Court of Appeal upheld the terminations for cause of two long-service management employees due to sexual harassment. In *Bannister v. General Motors of Canada Ltd.*[51], the Court found that a 20-year supervisor who engaged in pervasive inappropriate comments and conduct with female subordinates was properly terminated for cause. The Court of Appeal succinctly detailed its expectations for the workplace with the following statements:

> In an industrial plant, no one expects profanity or vulgarity to be eliminated, but unwelcome conduct or expressions based on gender or race cannot be tolerated. Management was entitled to have a supervisor who would do his best to assure that the environment was clear of racist or sexist slurs or objectionable conduct. In respect of gender issues, the [supervisor] failed management. Given the finding that he joined in these activities without later apology or acknowledgment, it is hard to imagine an alternative to termination which would not perpetuate the harassment which management was obligated to eliminate. In my view, the termination was fully justified.[52]

---

[49]   *L'Attiboudeaire v. Royal Bank* (1996), 131 D.L.R. (4th) 445 (Ont. C.A.).

[50]   See *Tse v. Trow Consulting Engineers Ltd.* (1995), 14 C.C.E.L. (2d) 132 (Ont. Gen. Div.) in which an employee who ran his hand down the side of a female co-worker's body and over her breast was found to have been wrongfully dismissed and *Quirola v. Xerox Canada Inc.* (1996), 16 C.C.E.L. (2d) 235 (Ont. Gen. Div.) in which consistent attempts to engage a subordinate in conversations about her sex life and providing unsolicited vulgar information about sexual prowess and practices did not constitute just cause for dismissal.

[51]   (1998), 40 O.R. (3d) 577 (Eng.) (Ont. C.A.).

[52]   *Ibid*, at 190.

A similar result followed in *Gonsalves v. Catholic Church Extension Society of Canada*[53] involving a 59-year-old supervisor with 22 years of service who had tried to start a sexual relationship with his assistant. His attentions included inappropriate remarks, sexual solicitations, as well as inappropriate touching, including a tight hug during which he fondled her breasts and, on another occasion, when he rubbed up against her leg. Of greatest concern was the supervisor's own admission that he knew that the conduct complained of was unacceptable and conceded that he did not need to be told so.

The Ontario Court of Appeal reconfirmed its lack of tolerance for sexual harassment in 2001 with its decision in *Simpson v. Consumers' Assn. of Canada*[54], which involved the executive director of a non-profit association with four years' service, who created a sexually-charged working environment, even though most of the inappropriate conduct took place off-site and after working hours. This termination for cause was also found to be fully justified on appeal. The message by the Ontario Court of Appeal to employers, in no uncertain terms, is that supervisors are expected to lead by example in keeping their workplaces harassment-free. Where supervisors not only fail to do so, but also engage in inappropriate behaviour themselves, their conduct will not be excused, particularly if there is no acknowledgment of wrongdoing.

---

[53] (1998), 164 D.L.R. (4th) 339 (Ont. C.A.).

[54] (2001), 57 O.R. (3d) 351 (Ont. C.A.), application for leave to appeal to SCC dimissed (2002), [2002] S.C.C.A. No. 83, 2002 CarswellOnt 2653 (S.C.C.).

♦

CHAPTER 2

FOCUS ON EMPLOYER RESPONSIBILITY

1. Far-Reaching Obligations of Employers

Employers have an obligation to prohibit and prevent harassment in employment situations and in the workplace. Employers are required to investigate such complaints of harassment when they arise. Questions may arise as to what constitutes "employment" and the "workplace": Is it limited to the activities on the physical property that is commonly understood to be the workplace? Is it limited to interactions between employees? What are employers' duties when third parties, such as suppliers or customers, harass employees or when employees harass third parties? Does the obligation apply exclusively with respect to employers or does it apply to independent contractors as well?

The answers to these questions are not straightforward, but the following will provide some useful guidelines to assist in evaluating an employer's obligations in dealing with conduct beyond interactions between employees, which occur at the workplace and during working hours. Employers need to know how far their obligations extend so they can take the appropriate preventative measures, and respond appropriately to atypical complaints of harassment. For their part, potential complainants need some guidance as to who can be properly targeted as a useful respondent to a complaint. Lawyers for employees might wish to cast their net as far as possible, but there are always additional expenses and delays involved when parties are named as respondents without merit.

2. Union Responsibilities

This book and this chapter in particular, focuses on the obligations of employers with respect to the prevention of harassment in the workplace, and to remedying incidents of harassment that may arise. It should be noted, however, that in unionized workplaces employers share responsibility for upholding the rights prescribed by human rights legislation with their union. A union can be independently liable or jointly and severally liable with an employer for damages for harassment in the workplace.
To quote an Ontario court,

> Discrimination in the work place is everybody's business. There can be no hierarchy of responsibility. There are no primary or secondary obligations to avoid discrimination and adverse effect discrimination; Companies, Unions and persons are all in a primary and equal position in a single line of defence against all types of discrimination. To conclude otherwise would fail to afford the *Human Rights Code* the broad purposive intent that is mandated.[1]

3. Organic Theory of Employer Responsibility

What if you are the most conscientious employer around and despite providing extensive training to employees, entirely unbeknownst to you, a rogue supervisor harasses a subordinate. Is the employer liable in these circumstances? Depending on the particular circumstances in the case, the answer may be "yes". Canadian law has developed to the point that an employer's lack of awareness and/or conscientiousness is no defence to the harassing acts of its employees. The primary reason for this is that human rights laws are remedial statutes. They are designed to "fix" the situation created by the discrimination or harassment, not to unduly punish the ha-

---

[1] *Gohm v. Domtar Inc.* (1992), 8 O.R. (3d) 65 (Ont. Div. Ct.), affirming (1990), 90 C.L.L.C. 17,027 (Ont. Bd. of Inquiry); *Renaud v. Central Okanagan School District No. 23*, [1992] 2 S.C.R. 970 (S.C.C.).

rassers. The ability to fix a situation created by sexual harassment lies primarily with the employer, not the harasser.

Commenting on the *Canadian Human Rights Act* applicable to federally regulated employers, the Supreme Court of Canada determined that it "contemplates the imposition of liability on employers for all acts of their employees in the course of employment".[2] If the employer was not liable, certain remedies available to complainants to counteract harassment, such as reinstatement, could not be implemented. While this is not precisely the same as vicarious liability, the concept is similar.

Ontario's *Human Rights Code* expressly excludes companies from the deemed liability that applies to the acts of its officers, officials, employees or agents when those acts involve harassment, including sexual solicitation and reprisal. Even so, adjudicators under the Code have developed an "organic theory of corporate responsibility" to find employers jointly and severally liable with their harassing employees. That is, where an employee in a position of authority is part of the "directing mind" of the employer, the corporate veil will be pierced so that the employer becomes responsible for that employee's acts and omissions.[3] Under the organic theory of corporate responsibility, the act of the employee becomes the act of the corporate entity itself.[4] Who, then, is part of the "directing mind" of an employer? Managers, directors and significant shareholders certainly will meet the test. In other situations it will be a question as to the authority, control and discretion wielded by the employee, if any, in respect of hiring, firing and discipline.

Employers should not lose heart that their efforts to prevent and stamp out harassment are in vain. There is an important distinction between employer liability and remedy. Even if an employer's conduct is irrelevant to the imposition of liability, it may have important practical implications when remedies are considered. To the extent that an employer takes appropriate measures, it may render redundant many of the contemplated remedies. As a result, an employer who responds promptly and effectively to a complaint, to remedy and prevent recurrence, will not be liable to the same extent, if at all, as an employer who does not do so.[5]

---

[2]   *Robichaud v. Brennan* (1987), 40 D.L.R. (4th) 577 (S.C.C.) at 584.

[3]   *Supra*, note 7.

[4]   *Olarte v. Commodore Business Machines Ltd.* (1983), 4 C.H.R.R. D/1705 (Ont. Bd. of Inquiry), affirmed (1984), 10 Admin. L.R. 130 (Ont. Div. Ct.) at D/1743-44 [C.H.R.R.].

[5]   *Supra*, note 6 at para. 19. See also *Wall v. Embro* (1995), 95 C.L.L.C. 230-029 (Ont. Bd. of Inquiry) [hereinafter *Wall*] in which the employer was found to have acted reasonably in its response to the complainant, including its rejection of certain demands made by the complainant such that

4. Conduct Occurring After-Hours and Off-Site

An employer's obligation to provide a workplace free from harassment, as recognized by human rights legislation, can extend beyond working hours and the workplace. Inappropriate conduct at a customer's cocktail party has been found to constitute sexual harassment.[6] Incidents in a hospitality suite at a sales convention, at a company retreat, and even at the boss's cottage that are perceived by employees to be job related, despite their social component, can also be the source of sexual harassment.[7] To quote the Ontario Court of Appeal, "It would be artificial and contrary to the purpose of controlling sexual harassment in the workplace to say that after-work interaction between a supervisor and other employees cannot constitute the workplace for the purpose of the application of the law regarding employment-related sexual harassment."[8]

5. Employees vs. Independent Contractors

We have seen that the definition of "employment" has been expanded to include occurrences that take place after working hours and off-site. The expansive definition of employment provokes the further question as to whether the protection from harassment is limited to employees or extended to those non-employees who also provide regular services in a workplace, such as independent contractors and volunteers. Not surprisingly, the definition of "employee" has been liberally interpreted by human rights tribunals to mean "to use the services of a person," such that an independent contractor has been entitled to the same freedom from discrimination and harassment as an employee.[9] It is also likely that a regular volunteer could claim the same protection. Employers are well advised to consider their obligation to provide a harassment-free workplace to apply to any individual who provides regular services.

---

its liability was limited to $3,500 in general damages for the psychological effects of a supervisor's harassment.

[6] *Tellier v. Bank of Montreal* (1987), 17 C.C.E.L. 1 (Ont. Dist. Ct.).

[7] *Supra*, note 55 and *Lengert v. Samuel* (1999), 99 C.L.L.C. 230-032 (B.C. Human Rights Trib.).

[8] *Supra*, note 55 at 371.

[9] See *Gordy v. Oak Bay MarinaMarine Management Ltd. v. British Columbia (Human Rights Commission)* (2000), [2000] B.C.H.R.T.D. No. 15, 2000 CarswellBC 2926 (B.C. Human Rights Trib.), reversed (2000), 39 C.H.R.R. D/8 (B.C. S.C.), reversed (2002), 43 C.H.R.R. D/487 (B.C. C.A.), in which an independent contractor fishing guide was found to be entitled to protection from discrimination based on disability.

6. Conduct Involving Third Parties

An employer's obligation to provide a workplace free from harassment, as recognized by human rights legislation, can extend to the conduct of employee *vis-à-vis* third parties, and the conduct of third parties *vis-à-vis* employees. Employers are responsible for ensuring that their employees are able to work in an environment free from harassment not only by superiors, subordinates and peers, but also by non-employees, such as, independent contractors, customers, suppliers, courier personnel and others who enter the workplace or deal with the employees. Further, employers are responsible for ensuring that their employees do not harass third parties who come in contact with their employees while they are working. It is a sound extension of anti-harassment policies to ensure that they govern all who are lawfully present at the workplace.

7. Case Analyses

As we indicated above, it is difficult to precisely define the parameters of the employment relationship within which employers will be responsible for the conduct of their employees. As such, reviewing some cases that have dealt with unusual employment situations should provide a better understanding of how decision-makers assess these situations.

7.a.   Tellier v. Bank of Montreal

Tellier v. Bank of Montreal[10] was one of the earliest decisions to find harassment that occurred outside working hours to be offensive, and to warrant cause for termination of employment. Tellier was a senior manager with over 18 years of service with the Bank. A female administrative employee complained of a number of incidents of inappropriate touching by Tellier. A number of these incidents occurred in the workplace; another occurred at a cocktail party held by a company that was doing business with the Bank. At the cocktail party, the complainant alleged that Tellier insisted on helping the complainant remove her name tag from her sweater and place it on the clothes she was wearing and, in doing so, touched her breast. After reviewing the allegations, the Bank terminated Tellier's employment for cause.

---

[10]   *Supra*, note 61.

The Court drew no distinction between the incidents that occurred on Bank premises during working hours, and the cocktail party incident, in finding that the Bank had no reasonable alternative but to terminate Tellier's employment.

7.b.　　Simpson v. Consumers' Association of Canada

Simpson v. Consumers' Assn.Association of Canada[11] also arises out of the termination of a senior manager for cause due to sexual harassment. In this case, Simpson was his employer's Executive Director. He reported directly to the Board of Directors. At trial, his conduct was excused by the trial judge who found him to be wrongfully dismissed and entitled to 18 months' pay and benefits. This decision was overturned in its entirety on appeal with the Ontario Court of Appeal delivering an important lesson for employers and employees on the definition of workplace and expectations of supervisors and managers.

The following six incidents demonstrate the impropriety of Simpson's conduct: (1) He suggested to his 22-year old secretary/executive assistant that opportunities could arise for her if she had a sexual relationship with him. When she refused, he became unpleasant and sarcastic towards her, triggering her resignation. (2) He took employer's legal counsel out for a drink after a business meeting outside the office, and tricked her into going to a strip club, and engaged her in a sexual discussion. He continued these sexual discussions during a business trip. (3) He had an affair with his secretary, which was obvious to everyone in the office. (4) He invited his secretary, legal counsel and another employee to his cottage to discuss business matters. After the discussion Simpson and his secretary went skinny-dipping. (5) While attending an out-of-town board meeting, Simpson undressed and entered a hot tub in front of other employees. His secretary entered the hot tub bare-breasted. (6) In a hospitality suite, again out-of-town, he grabbed an employee's buttocks. When another employee complained, he apologized but later fired the employee who had complained.

Three of the incidents took place at meetings or retreats held at hotels and clearly had a social component. The Court of Appeal found, however, that the timing of the incidents after the end of official business meetings did not mean that they were outside the workplace and the employment context. The test applied by the Court of Appeal was whether the employees perceived the situations to be job related. To the extent that employees

---

[11]　*Supra,* note 55.

24

attended a function outside the physical confines of the office and outside working hours because it was job related, the incidents that occurred there were found to take place in the context of the work environment.

7.c.   Lanteigne v. Sam's Sports Bar Ltd. (c.o.b. G.G.'s Sports Bar)

In *Lanteigne v. Sam's Sports Bar Ltd.*[12], a waitress at a bar alleged that she had been sexually harassed by a regular patron who grabbed her breast as he left the bar. The waitress claimed to have gone immediately to the manager to inform him of the incident. The manager claimed not to recall any complaint by the waitress directly that night, but that he learned of the incident at a staff meeting a few days later. The waitress complained that her subsequent dismissal was motivated by her requests that management establish a sexual harassment policy to deal with misconduct by customers.

The British Columbia Human Rights Tribunal determined that although the employer was not directly responsible for the sexual harassment, it had an obligation to protect its employees from sexual harassment by its customers. The Tribunal added that the employer, when informed that a customer of its establishment had sexually harassed an employee, was obliged to take some action. In this case, the employer took no action upon being informed about the incident of sexual harassment, and subsequently treated the waitress's concerns lightly. Further, the Tribunal found, in fact, that it was waitress's request for an all-encompassing sexual harassment policy that led to her dismissal. The waitress was awarded $3,000 as compensation for injury to dignity, feelings and self-respect. Additionally, the employer was ordered to develop a sexual harassment policy that would cover the conduct of patrons at the bar, as well as employees.

7.d.   Mahmoodi v. University of British Columbia

In *Mahmoodi v. University of British Columbia*[13], the complainant alleged that, while she was a student at the University of British Columbia ("UBC"), she was sexually harassed by one of her professors, Dutton. The complainant met Dutton at his home for two meetings. It was undisputed that at both meetings Dutton served wine, candles were lit and music was

---

[12]   (1998), *Lanteigne v. Sam's Sports Bar Ltd. (c.o.b. G.G.'s Sports Bar)*, [1998] B.C.H.R.T.D. No. 40, 98 C.L.L.C. 230-045 (B.C. Human Rights Trib.)(B.C.H.R.T.).

[13]   *Mahmoodi v. University of British Columbia, supra,* note 8.

playing. Further, at the second meeting, Dutton prepared dinner for the complainant.

The complainant alleged that during the second visit to Dutton's home, he kissed her and touched her breasts. At the time of this encounter, the complainant had been seeking admission to graduate school and was hopeful that Dutton would provide her with assistance with her application. Dutton denied any touching, kissing, fondling or dancing, or any sexual element in respect of any of his dealings with the complainant. The complainant complained to UBC of the events, and UBC investigated the allegations. An investigation report concluded that, "Dutton had engaged in professional misconduct and a breach of professional ethics, although his actions did not include overt sexual interaction". A disciplinary letter was placed in Dutton's personnel file.

The complainant still filed a human rights complaint. The British Columbia Human Rights Tribunal concluded that sexual harassment had occurred. The Tribunal commented that Dutton created and controlled a sexualized environment beyond the normal professional boundaries between a professor and a student. As Dutton's employer, UBC was held to be vicariously liable for his acts. Accordingly, Dutton and UBC were found jointly and severally liable to pay the complainant over $12,000 in damages, which included approximately $5,000 for counselling, $4,000 for injury to feelings, and $3,000 for lost wages.

In this case, the employer was held liable for the acts of its employee even though they occurred outside of the employment relationship; that is, *vis-à-vis* a third party student, as well as outside of the workplace.

◆

CHAPTER 3

HOW TO DRAFT AND IMPLEMENT ANTI-HARASSMENT POLICIES

1. The Anti-Harassment Policy:
A Communication Tool and a General Warning

The anti-harassment policy is an excellent tool for communicating the employer's position in respect of harassment in the workplace. The policy also serves as a means of warning employees that they will be subject to discipline for engaging in harassing comments or conduct. In other words, the policy essentially serves as a written warning to all employees about the employer's expectations in respect of proper conduct during work and associated activities. A well-written anti-harassment policy is effective in reducing the employer's potential liability in the face of a claim, as these kinds of policies are taken into account by human rights tribunals in assessing the appropriate remedies. In fact, the *Canada Labour Code* makes it mandatory for federally regulated employers to have a policy statement regarding sexual harassment, and specifies the contents of the policy statement.[1]

---

[1] *Canada Labour Code*, R.S.C. 1985, c. L-2, s. 247, 4.

27

As we have noted, harassment, if based on prohibited grounds, can be viewed as a particular form of unlawful discrimination. For this reason, many employers include the anti-harassment policy as part of their human rights policy. Other employers prefer to have two separate policies. The human rights policy tends to focus on the employer's commitment to equal opportunity in the workplace and the avoidance of unlawful discrimination. The anti-harassment policy focuses on each individual's right to be respected by other workplace players, and to be free from the unwelcome abuse, solicitation and threats that are part of a poisoned workplace in general, and specific situations of harassment in particular.

2. Zero Tolerance Policies

It is important to make a comment at this point about "zero tolerance" policies, which provide that, if the misconduct is established, then the consequence will always be dismissal. "Zero tolerance" policies have become fashionable in recent years, particularly for U.S.-based employers, to demonstrate the seriousness of management's commitment to preventing harassment in the workplace.

While the high standards and expectations emphasized by a zero tolerance policy are valuable, the zero tolerance concept and terminology are not useful in a Canadian employment context. For an employer to terminate an employee, whether unionized or not, for just cause, it must meet a high standard. Although sexual harassment may meet that standard in some cases, it will not meet it in all. Whether before an arbitrator for unionized employees, or before the courts for non-union employees, the law expects that each situation will be carefully considered and determined on its own facts, including mitigating factors such as the employee's age, length of service, disciplinary record and surrounding circumstances. Even where dismissal appears to be the likely consequence, there should always be the possibility that, in the right circumstances, the employer might use its discretion to come to a different result. Employers should have high standards and, therefore, a very low tolerance for situations of sexual harassment. However, what zero tolerance really means is that the employer is giving away its managerial discretion.

3. Key Elements of an Anti-Harassment Policy

The key elements that should be included in a well-written anti-harassment policy include the following:

- A statement about the employer's policy;
- A definition of the misconduct covered by the policy;
- A statement about the employer's intentions in respect of proper conduct after-hours and involving third parties;
- A statement about the responsibilities of the different workplace players;
- A complaint procedure for persons who consider themselves victims of prohibited misconduct;
- An outline of the investigation procedure to deal with complaints under the policy;
- Identification of the consequences for those responsible for violations of the policy;
- The time for filing a complaint; and
- The consequences of filing a malicious or frivolous complaint.

These key elements are reviewed in further detail immediately below. Workplaces that do not have a policy at present should be able to build a customized policy directly from these pages. Workplaces that have a policy in place should be able to review and revise that policy to ensure that each of these key elements is appropriately addressed. Policies and practices in respect of human rights and anti-harassment should be reviewed and revised, including appropriate training, on a regular annual basis.

3.a.   Policy Statement

An anti-harassment policy should include a policy statement acknowledging the employer's commitment to providing a workplace free from harassment, in accordance with human rights legislation. The policy statement should also state that harassing conduct, in contravention of the policy, will not be tolerated.

Employers may wish to strive to achieve a workplace that is free from all forms of harassment. However, it is unnecessary and unwise to include such a broad statement in the policy. By including a broad statement in the policy to the effect that all forms of harassment are prohibited, employers risk imposing on themselves a higher onus of responsibility and liability than would otherwise be required. However, the current trend appears to be that employers are also including "personal harassment" in their policy, and this is probably advisable now that the courts are recognizing claims for intentional infliction of mental suffering and constructive dismissal. Trivial complaints of personal harassment can be easily dismissed under the terms of the policy.

3.b. Definition

An anti-harassment policy should include a definition of what constitutes harassment. It is important that employees understand that the misconduct in question is a personal offence by one employee against another person, whether or not an employee or a third party in the workplace setting. The definition should list the grounds of prohibited harassment consistent with those in human rights legislation, and a clear definition of personal harassment, if you choose to include it within your policy. In addition, examples of harassment should be included to ensure that employees understand the type of conduct in issue.

Some forms of harassment may require repetition before they violate the legislation in a strict legal sense. Most employers do not want to wait that long, especially if the impugned conduct involves a relationship between a superior and a subordinate employee. The anti-harassment policy should indicate that a single incident of misconduct may violate the policy. Employees should be encouraged to come forward with complaints, even if there is no evidence of repeated conduct.

The concept of a poisoned work environment also should be explained. This will help employees understand that even if their conduct is not directed at a particular person, it can still poison the workplace environment for members of an identifiable group who could be expected to take offence.

3.c. After-Hours Conduct and Third Party Dealings

The anti-harassment policy should make it clear to employees that they are required to comply with the policy, both during and after work hours, and at or away from the workplace, when associating with co-workers in activities that are directly related to the employer's business. This can include, for example, attending company sponsored events and business trips. Employers should consider including the *caveat* that the policy is not designed to intrude into the private affairs of individuals and does not extend beyond working hours or the workplace, except in respect of activities that have a connection to work and to the business of the employer, or which could adversely impact the relationship at the workplace.

The anti-harassment policy should inform employees that they are expected to abide by the policy in all of their exchanges with third parties with whom they deal in the course of their employment, such as customers, suppliers and couriers. The anti-harassment policy also should inform employees that third parties with whom they deal in the course of their employment are prohibited from harassing them, and that the employer will take action to investigate and stop any such harassment. Even if the employer takes on greater liability with such a statement, if it is serious about preventing harassment and a poisoned work environment, the employer must expect proper conduct from and towards any individual who has legitimate access to the workplace.

3.d.   Responsibilities

The policy should make it clear that it is everyone's responsibility to ensure that the workplace is free from harassment in accordance with human rights legislation. This means that everyone has a duty to comply with and ensure compliance with the anti-harassment policy. All employees should be encouraged to report any incidents of harassing conduct to management, regardless of whether the conduct was directed at them or not.

The policy should make it clear that any member of management who witnesses harassing conduct that may contravene human rights legislation is authorized to deal with the situation, whether or not the member of management is responsible for any of the employees involved, and whether or not there is a formal complaint.

3.e.   Discipline, Reprisals and Liability

Employees should be advised that their failure to comply with the policy could result in discipline, up to and including immediate dismissal from their employment, for just cause. Further, employees should be made aware that they risk personal liability for monetary damages as a result of their harassing conduct or comments.

The anti-harassment policy should state that employees will not be subject to discipline or reprisals for making complaints of harassment or providing evidence about a complaint. The only exception to that protection is if an employee files a frivolous or malicious complaint, or is intentionally dishonest in a material way, which is bad faith.

3.f.   Complaint Procedure

The anti-harassment policy should explain how employees can make a complaint of harassment and to whom such a complaint should be made. Employees should be informed of their option of making a complaint to their direct superior or human resources, or any other managerial employee with whom they feel comfortable, without fear of criticism or reprisal if they bypass their direct superior.

The policy should request that the complaint be made in writing. Employers can provide employees with a complaint form, but it is not required. Employees should be advised that any complaint that is made, even if it is not in writing, may prompt an investigation.

A sample complaint form is included at the end of this chapter. This sample should be reviewed carefully and revised as necessary to suit the unique needs of each employer. In particular, if a form is developed, it should specify the grounds of harassment prohibited in the jurisdiction in which the employer operates. A national form is possible for employers that are covered by multiple jurisdictions, so long as the different terms used in the different jurisdictions are included to comprehensively describe the prohibited grounds.

The policy should encourage employees to bring forward complaints of harassment as soon as possible. Timely complaints will assist employers in addressing any problems at the first possible opportunity and preventing any further harassment. In addition, timely complaints will enable the employer to better assess the credibility of those involved while the events in issue are still fresh in their minds.

The information published by some of the provincial human rights commissions suggests that employees should be advised of their right to file complaints with the human rights commission, even if they have filed internal complaints. Employers should carefully consider whether or not they want to incorporate this right into their own policies. It is sufficient to simply post the information material that is readily available from each human rights commission. If the policy does notify employees of their right to file complaints under human rights legislation, it should also notify employees of any time limits within which to file such complaints. The time limits vary across jurisdictions and some jurisdictions are without any express time limitation at all. Where there is a time limit, that limit varies by jurisdiction from six to twenty-four months from the date of the last incident.[2]

3.g.   Investigation Procedure

The anti-harassment policy should outline what happens once the employer receives the complaint. The policy should state that the employer will investigate complaints of harassment that are made in good faith, and report back to the complainant in a timely manner.

The policy should advise employees that the investigation may include a meeting with the alleged harasser and any potential witnesses. The policy should state that the investigation process is confidential, but that the employer will be required to disclose information to the extent necessary to conduct the investigation. The policy should remind everyone involved in the investigation to keep the matter confidential and not to discuss it with co-workers. It should be made clear that wilful breaches of confidentiality may also become subject to disciplinary action.

4.   Implementing Anti-Harassment Policies

Employers must ensure their anti-harassment policy is properly implemented in order for it to be effective. From the outset, this involves developing the policy through consultation, input and feedback from those who will be affected by the policy, including employees, representatives from the union or employee association, if any, and managers.

Leadership is also important to ensure the successful implementation of the policy. Senior management must support the policy and, more impor-

---

[2]   No time limit is found in Nova Scotia's *Human Rights Act*, R.S.N.S. 1989, c. 214; Nunavut and the Northwest Territories' *Fair Practices Act*, R.S.N.W.T. 1988, c. F-2. A six-month time limit is found in British Columbia's *Human Rights Code*, R.S.B.C. 1996, c. 210, s. 22; Manitoba's *Human Rights Code*, C.C.S.M., c. H175, c. 45, s. 23; Newfoundland and Labrador's *Human Rights Code*, R.S.N. 1990, c. H-14, s. 20(2); Ontario's *Human Rights Code*, R.S.O. 1990, c. H.19, s. 34(1); and the Yukon's *Human Rights Act*, R.S.Y. 2002, c. 116, s. 20(2). Discretion to allow extensions is available in British Columbia, Manitoba and Ontario. A 12-month time limit is found in Alberta's *Human Rights, Citizenship and Multiculturalism Act*, R.S.A. 2000, c. H-14, s. 20(2); the federal *Canadian Human Rights Act*, R.S.C. 1985, c. H-6, s. 41; New Brunswick's *Human Rights Act*, R.S.N.B. 1973, c. H-11, s. 17.1; and Prince Edward Island's *Human Rights Act*, R.S.P.E.I. 1988, c. H-12, s. 22(2). Extensions may be granted in the federal jurisdiction and New Brunswick. A two-year discretionary time limit is provided by Quebec's *Charter of Human Rights and Freedoms*, R.S.Q. 1977, c. C-12, s. 77. A two-year time limit, without discretion, is provided by the Saskatchewan *Human Rights Code*, S.S. 1979, c. S-24.1, s. 27(5).

tantly, it must be seen to be supported by senior management, who take the issue seriously and demonstrate a proud corporate commitment to providing a harassment-free workplace.

The policy should be communicated to new hires from the outset of their employment. To ensure that a newly hired employee has received and reviewed the policy, employees should be required to sign an acknowledgment confirming that they have read the policy, understand it and will abide by it. By having the employee sign two copies of the acknowledgment, the employee can keep one for his or her own file, and the employer can keep the other one.

Employees should be reminded on a regular basis of the employer's commitment to providing a harassment-free workplace in accordance with its policy. This might take the form of annual newsletters to employees, or annual meetings with employees at which the policy is reviewed and attendance is taken. If the employer chooses the same time of each calendar year to review and revise the policy and to affect a renewed communication strategy with employees, then it can be reasonably sure to be current and to appear to be concerned about preventing harassment and promoting a positive working environment.

The policy should be easily accessible to employees, so that it can be reviewed at any time. This could include posting the policy on the employer's intranet site, posting copies on bulletin boards, printing it in an up-to-date employee handbook, and maintaining the policy with all of the other policies in a central area accessible to employees. These methods of communication are not mutually exclusive; at least one such method should be used, if not all of them.

Having a policy that employees do not know about is akin to not having a policy at all. Proper implementation and regular communication reminding employees of the policy is critical to its effectiveness. We also encourage periodic training at all levels of the organization.

5. Sample Anti-Harassment Policies

The following are sample anti-harassment policies intended as reference tools. Employers will need to revise and adapt these sample policies to develop their own policy that meets the needs of their organizations.

SAMPLE ANTI-HARASSMENT POLICY # 1

Policy Statement

<The Organization>, in co-operation with our Union, is committed to ensuring employees work in a harassment-free environment, in accordance with human rights legislation. Accordingly, <the Organization> prohibits harassment based on race, place of origin, colour, ethnic origin, citizenship, creed, age, marital status, family status, disability, record of offences, sex and sexual orientation, as defined by the human rights legislation governing our workplace, and any other prohibited grounds of harassment included in such legislation. These are collectively referred to as the "prohibited grounds" of harassment.

Definition of Harassment

Harassment occurs when an employee is subjected to unwelcome verbal or physical conduct from another employee based on the prohibited grounds of harassment, described above.

The following are examples of harassment:

- Derogatory remarks about a person's religious beliefs;
- Jokes about a person's place of origin;
- The display of racist or offensive images;
- Offensive comments about a person's age or physical appearance; and
- Mimicking.

It is important to understand that harassment can occur whether or not the inappropriate comments or conduct occurs directly to another person, face-to-face, or in the absence of the other person, behind his or her back.

Definition of Sexual Harassment

Sexual harassment, being discrimination on the grounds of gender, is a violation of human rights legislation. Unwanted sexual advances, unwanted requests for sexual favours, and other unwanted verbal or physical conduct of a sexual nature constitute sexual harassment when:

1. Submission to such conduct is made either explicitly or implicitly a term of, or condition of, an individual's employment; or
2. Submission to, or rejection of such conduct by any individual affects that individual's employment.

Sexual harassment can include such things as pinching, patting, rubbing or leering, "dirty" jokes, pictures or pornographic materials, comments, suggestions, innuendos, requests or demands of a sexual nature. The behaviour need not be intentional in order to be considered sexual harassment.

Discipline

Harassment that is prohibited by human rights legislation will not be tolerated within <the Organization>. Employees who engaged in such misconduct may be subject to discipline up to and including discharge.

Procedure

If you are being harassed:

1. If you feel that you are able to do so, tell the harasser that his/her behaviour is unwelcome and ask him/her to stop.
2. If you are unable to speak to the harasser or if the behaviour continues even after your have asked him/her to stop, or at any time you feel you are being harassed, report the problem to your boss, human resources, union representative, or any member of management with whom you feel comfortable.
3. You also have the right to contact the Human Rights Commission to file a complaint of harassment within the required time limit, which is [TIME], in this province.
4. Finally, if circumstances warrant it, a charge of assault may be filed with the police.

Dealing with a Complaint

1. Once a complaint is received, it will be kept confidential, to the extent possible, subject to <the Organization's> duty to investigate.
2. Both the complainant and the alleged harasser may be interviewed, as will any individuals who may be able to provide relevant information.
3. If the investigation reveals evidence to support the complaint of harassment, the harasser will be disciplined appropriately. Discipline may in-

clude suspension without pay or dismissal, and the incident will be documented in the harasser's file.

4. Regardless of the outcome of a harassment complaint made in good faith, the employee lodging the complaint, as well as anyone providing information, will be protected from any form of retaliation by either co-workers or superiors.

Responsibilities of Employees

All employees are responsible for complying with this policy and maintaining the harassment-free workplace. This obligation extends to the dealings of employees with third parties, such as customers, suppliers and delivery personnel. This obligation also extends to after-hours business meetings or trips, or other events sponsored by <the Organization>.

The Organization seeks to provide a safe, healthy and rewarding work environment for its employees. **Harassment will not be tolerated within <this Organization>!** If you feel you are being harassed, contact us. We want to hear from you.

SAMPLE ANTI-HARASSMENT POLICY #2

Introduction

The purpose of this policy is to make all employees, including management, aware of <the Organization's> position on harassment in the workplace. Human rights legislation makes it unlawful for anyone in the course of his or her employment to harass anyone on the basis of age, race, ancestry, place of origin, colour, ethnic origin, citizenship, creed, sex, sexual orientation, marital status, same-sex partnership status, family status, disability or record of offences. These are the prohibited grounds of harassment.

<The Company> is firmly committed to preserving and maintaining a work environment that is free from harassment in accordance with human rights legislation. It is the responsibility of each member of staff and management to foster and encourage such an environment, and to take appropriate steps in the event of a contravention of this policy. <The Company> will investigate and respond to a complaint of harassment and will take remedial action as necessary and appropriate, including disciplinary action up to and including dismissal.

Definition of Harassment

Harassment has been defined as: "engaging in a course of vexatious comment or conduct that is known or ought reasonably to be known to be unwelcome". There could be circumstances in which a single incident of inappropriate behaviour by an employee may be substantial enough to constitute a breach of human rights legislation, by creating a "poisoned environment". Even if the comments or conduct are not directed at any one person, someone may still experience a poisoned environment because she or he is also a member of the group targeted.

Harassment based on sex consists of inappropriate comments and actions of a sexual nature, or based on a person's gender. Every employee, staff and member of management is entitled to be free of personal invitations, advances or sexual solicitations from fellow employees, clients of <the Company>, and from someone who is in a position to exercise any control over his or her income, job security or other conditions of employment, if the person extending the invitation or making the advance or solicitation knows or ought reasonably to know that it is unwelcome.

The following are examples of sexual harassment:

- Jokes or comments about sex, sexual preferences and sexual matters;
- Touching or patting;
- Standing or sitting unduly close to someone;
- Use of derogatory language that is gender-biased;
- Inquiries or comments about an individual's sex life; and
- The display of sexually offensive material, including displays *via* e-mail, internet or otherwise.

Employees are responsible for complying with this policy in their dealings with employees and third parties while in the course of their employment. This applies to conduct while at work, during business meetings, on business trips and at company events.

<The Company> will treat harassment as a serious contravention of the conditions of employment. <The Company> will investigate and respond to a complaint of harassment, and will take whatever remedial action as is necessary and appropriate, including disciplinary action up to and including dismissal.

While this policy does not mean that social interaction between people who work together is prohibited, it requires that all employees, and particularly those who exercise influence over the income, working conditions and job security of others, be sensitive to the restraints required in the conduct of their working relationships with fellow employees.

Complaint Procedure

Harassment complaints should be made to **[insert contact position],** or any other member of management with whom you feel comfortable. <The Company> will then conduct an investigation of the matter.

Any person who receives a complaint or becomes aware of a contravention of this policy, whether formally or informally, should promptly refer the matter to **[insert contact position]**.

<The Company> has an obligation to investigate complaints of harassment, as protected by human rights legislation. <The Company> will endeavour to respect the confidentiality of a complainant and the person about whom the complaint was made to the extent possible in keeping with <the Company's> obligation to investigate. In order to complete the investigation, discussions among the investigator, the person complained about,

witnesses and legal counsel might be necessary. Anyone who participates in an investigation must respect the confidentiality of those involved in the complaint process as well. There will be no reprisals against an employee who, in good faith, makes a complaint.

SAMPLE HARASSMENT COMPLAINT FORM

Name: _____

Position: _____

Date Submitted: _____

Ground(s) of Harassment Claimed: *[please check the appropriate ground(s)]*

❏ Race	❏ Ancestry	❏ Place of origin
❏ Colour	❏ Ethnic origin	❏ Citizenship
❏ Creed	❏ Age	❏ Record of offences
❏ Marital status	❏ Same-sex partnership status	❏ Family status
❏ Disability	❏ Sex	❏ Other

Explanation: *[Explain the allegations, including who the allegations are against, the date and time of the incident(s), where the incident(s) occurred and the names of any witnesses to the incident(s). You may attached additional pages as required.]*

_____   _____

Signature of Employee   **Received By** *[insert name and title]*

♦

CHAPTER 4

WHAT TO DO UPON RECEIPT OF A COMPLAINT

1. Basic Principles

Employers should be prepared to deal with complaints of harassment in the workplace, and to react to conduct that constitutes harassment, even if there is no formal complaint. Having a "plan of action" in place ahead of time will ensure that harassment complaints and inappropriate conduct will be dealt with in a prompt and effective manner. The existence and suitable activation of such a plan of action will further reduce liability exposure for the employer, as well as for the individuals who are required to deal with the issue. A plan of action that is well drafted and that is followed in the event of a situation is not a complete answer, but its mere existence is a good start.

Employers, managers and supervisors must respond promptly upon receiving a complaint of harassment. Even when a formal complaint is not made, if any manager or supervisor becomes aware of harassing conduct in the workplace, that manager or supervisor should stop the misconduct if it is ongoing and bring all such misconduct to the attention of human resources or more senior management, who will assess how to proceed. This responsibility to react and report exists whether or not the aggressor was directing the misconduct towards the manager or supervisor, and whether or not there is a direct supervisory relationship in place.

2. The Importance of a Written Complaint

If the complainant makes a complaint orally, it is important to get the allegations in writing. This can be done by asking the complainant to put the complaint in writing. Alternatively, if the complainant does not want to put the complaint in writing, has difficulty articulating the complaint or refuses to do so, the employer should restate the oral complaint in writing and ask the complainant to sign an acknowledgment that the employer's statement accurately reflects what he or she has said. In order to handle a complaint properly, it is important to define all of the allegations and to confirm the complainant's agreement with that definition. Those allegations will then allow for an appropriate assessment of the complaint.

3. Preliminary Assessment of the Complaint

Upon receipt of a complaint regarding workplace conduct, the employer must assess whether it should commence a formal investigation. Not all complaints require a formal investigation, and nothing will be gained by commencing a formal investigation where one is not required. Indeed, much can be lost by conducting an unnecessary investigation; investigations are costly, and can create workplace disruptions and tension. It may be possible to resolve matters that do not warrant a formal investigation by meeting with the employees involved and discussing the issues to the point of a mutually satisfactory resolution.

The following are four preliminary questions that an employer should consider in assessing whether or not to conduct a formal investigation.

3.a. Is it Prohibited Harassment?

First, in assessing whether a formal investigation is required, the employer must consider whether or not the alleged conduct complained of, if it turns out to be true, could be a prohibited ground of harassment. In making this assessment, employers should look at their anti-harassment policy. If the employee is a unionized employee, there may be provisions governing harassment in the collective agreement. Does the anti-harassment policy or collective agreement, if any, protect employees from all forms of harassment, or only those prohibited grounds of harassment recognized by human rights legislation? If the alleged conduct appears to fall within the grounds of prohibited harassment that the employer recognizes, then the employer will need to examine the situation further.

If the alleged conduct does not appear to be covered by a policy, the collective agreement or human rights law, the employer still should consider means of resolving the issues raised in the complaint, other than commencing a formal investigation. Working environments with fractured relationships between managers and subordinates who felt unfairly criticized for reasons other than prohibited harassment have led to findings of constructive dismissal.[1] Aside from the desire to create a positive, harassment-free environment designed to enable employees to work to their full potential, this is another good reason why an employer should review carefully allegations of harassment even on non-prohibited grounds. Some form of action, although not necessarily a formal investigation, still may be in an employer's best interests.

3.b. Is it Prohibited Harassment in Employment?

Second, the employer must assess whether the alleged conduct constitutes prohibited harassment in employment, assuming that the allegations are true. As previously discussed, the employer's obligation to investigate allegations of harassment extends to its employees and third parties who come in contact with its employees in the course of their employment. This may include situations that have a work connection that occur away from the workplace and after-hours.

If a complaint of harassment is received from someone other than an employee, or made against someone other than an employee, the employer should assess whether it has any obligation to investigate. If the complaint appears to fall within the employment context, even though it involves non-employees, at least in part, the employer should continue its assessment. If the complaint falls entirely outside the employment context, the employer should not proceed with an investigation. Rather, the employer should assess whether there is any point in it becoming involved in the situation, so as to assist in a resolution, or whether doing so creates poten-

---

[1] *Shah v. Xerox Canada Ltd.* (1998), 49 C.C.E.L. (2d) 30 (Ont. Gen. Div.), affirmed (2000), 49 C.C.E.L. (2d) 166 (Ont. C.A.); *Prinzo v. Baycrest Centre for Geriatric Care* (2002), 60 O.R. (3d) 474 (Ont. C.A.).

tial liability. Employers should proceed with caution when making this assessment because if the complainant has complained to the employer about harassing conduct, there may be a reason, even if not obvious on the "face" of the complaint, why the complainant notified the employer. The employer may well find itself involved in a much bigger problem by failing to take action, especially if there appears to be a good possibility that its intervention might achieve a prompt and effective resolution of whatever it is that gave rise to the complaint.

3.c.   Is the Complaint Timely?

Third, in assessing whether the employer should proceed with a formal investigation into the complaint, the employer should consider the timeliness of the complaint. In evaluating the delay in bringing forward the complaint, the employer should take into account the time limit for filing a complaint under the applicable human rights legislation. As previously mentioned in Chapter 3, the time limit for filing complaints in most jurisdictions varies from six to twenty-four months.

Although the time limit for filing complaints under human rights legislation serves as a useful guide, it is not determinative of the employer's obligations. Generally, the time limits for filing complaints under human rights legislation may be extended and harassment in the workplace, whenever it occurred, needs to be addressed in some fashion, even if other than in a formal investigation. Nonetheless, if the complaint is filed far beyond a time limit set out in the applicable human rights legislation and the employer is prejudiced because of the delay, whether through a loss of witnesses or documents, it may be impossible to conduct a thorough, formal investigation.

3.d.   Is the Complaint Frivolous or Vexatious?

Fourth, with the exception of the Atlantic provinces[2], human rights legislation across Canada allows human rights commissions to dismiss complaints without proceeding to investigation where the allegations are determined to be "trivial, frivolous, vexatious or made in bad faith". Similarly, a formal investigation may not be required by an employer in

---

[2]   Human rights legislation in Newfoundland and Labrador, Nova Scotia, Prince Edward Island and New Brunswick does not permit their respective human rights commissions to not deal with complaints based on a determination that the complaint is trivial, frivolous, vexatious or made in bad faith.

these jurisdictions where the allegations, on their face, are clearly frivolous or obviously motivated by an improper purpose. Often some form of inquiry will be necessary to reach a conclusion on this issue and employers should keep in mind that human rights commissions are very reluctant to dismiss complaints on this basis. However, there will be rare cases that fit this description. These cases require a resolution other than a formal investigation; often a serious and measured response by the employer is sufficient. An example of such a situation would be an employee who files repeated complaints against her supervisor alleging no substantively new facts after the employer previously determined there was no merit to her initial complaint.

4. Due Diligence in Deciding Not to Deal With Complaints on Preliminary Grounds

Employers must exercise due diligence before deciding not to proceed with a formal investigation as a result of any of the grounds revealed by a preliminary inquiry. Employers must ensure that they fully understand the allegations and the nature of the complaint in making the preliminary assessments. Further, where there is any uncertainty about whether to proceed with a formal investigation, employers should err on the side of caution and conduct an investigation, which may turn out to have been unnecessary, rather than decide not to deal with a complaint on a preliminary ground. It is recommended that an employer seek external, professional advice in making these threshold determinations, in case a human rights investigator, commission or adjudicator later disagrees with the employer's assessment. Consulting an external expert will demonstrate the employer's due diligence in its assessment and will help to ensure that the employer makes a reasonable decision.

5. Complaints with Allegations of Criminal Conduct

It is quite possible that the allegations of harassment raised by a complainant may amount to criminal conduct. The *Criminal Code*[3] prohibits criminal harassment, uttering threats, assault, sexual assault and aggravated sexual assault. Criminal harassment[4] consists of knowingly or recklessly

---

[3]   *Criminal Code*, R.S.C. 1985, c. C-46.

[4]   *Ibid*, s. 264.

engaging in the following conduct, which causes the other person to fear for his or her safety or the safety of anyone known to him or her:

- Repeatedly following from place to place the person, or anyone known to them.
- Repeatedly communicating with the person, or anyone known to them.
- Besetting, watching the person, or anyone known to them, where he or she resides, works, carries on business or happens to be.
- Engaging in threatening conduct directed at the person, or any member of their immediate family.

Uttering threats involves knowingly uttering, conveying or causing any person to receive a threat to cause death or serious bodily harm.[5]
Assault under the *Criminal Code*[6] means a person:

- Without the consent of another person, applies force intentionally to that other person, directly or indirectly;
- Attempts or threatens, by an act or a gesture, to apply force to another person, if he or she has, or causes that other person to believe on reasonable grounds that he or she has, present ability to effect this purpose; or
- While openly wearing or carrying a weapon or an imitation thereof, accosts or impedes another person or begs.

A "sexual assault" is an assault that is committed in circumstances of a sexual nature such that the sexual integrity of the victim is violated. The part of the body touched, the nature of the contact, the situation in which it occurred, the words and gestures accompanying the act, and all of the circumstances surrounding the conduct, including threats, which may or may not be accompanied by force and the motive of the aggressor are relevant factors in determining whether the conduct was sexual.[7]

If these are the situations underlying the complaint, the employer should inform the complainant that he or she has alleged conduct that may constitute an offence under the *Criminal Code*, which may warrant notification to the police authorities. The employer should ask the complainant whether he or she intends to notify the police authorities. If the complainant does not notify the police authorities, the employer should consider whether it should do so. Where the allegations are of such a serious nature, this decision should not be taken lightly.

---

[5]   *Ibid*, s. 264.1(1)(a).

[6]   *Ibid*, s. 265.

[7]   *Ibid*, s. 271; *R. v. Chase* (1987), 37 C.C.C. (3d) 97 (S.C.C.).

Further, the employer must be cautious to ensure that its investigation does not compromise any action that may be required by the police authorities. It should be noted that it is an abuse of process and potentially extortion for an employer to use the threat of criminal charges as a self-help remedy to terminate an accused's employment.[8] An employer should not threaten to file or to refrain from filing criminal charges in order to secure the accused's resignation, release or any other civil remedy. If the employer is uncertain of its duties in these situations, it should seek external, professional advice.

6. The Employment Status of the Complainant Upon Submitting the Complaint

Both the incidents giving rise to a complaint and the act of making the complaint itself can impact on the complainant's desire and even ability to continue a "normal" employment relationship, at least while the investigation is underway and until the point of resolution. Following are the most common situations that can occur if the complainant does not feel able to continue working, pending resolution of the complaint.

6.a. Termination of Employment

There will be situations in which the complainant feels unable to continue in employment and there is no real expectation of a return to work at the conclusion of the investigation or at all. Hopefully this does not occur before the investigation is even commenced. This is not for the employer to say, but the employee may well communicate to the employer from the outset, either that he or she feels that the situation amounts to a constructive dismissal, or simply that he or she feels unable to continue in employment under the circumstances and is therefore resigning. Indeed, it may be in the course of an exit interview that the employer first finds out that harassment underlies the reason for the departure.

Assuming that the employer is unable, or does not try, to dissuade the employee from leaving, consideration should be given to negotiating a settlement that would include a release of all claims, including those under human rights law. If the employee is represented by a trade union, the un-

---

[8]   See, for example, *R. v. M.P.* (June 3, 1996), Reinhardt Prov. J., [1996] O.J. No. 2741 (Ont. Prov. Div.); *Criminal Code, supra*, note 73 at s. 346; *Rules of Professional Conduct*, Law Society of Upper Canada, rule 4.01(2)(l).

ion must be involved in any such negotiations. Indeed, even if the employee would prefer to keep the trade union out of it, under basic labour relations principles, it is inappropriate for employers to bargain directly with employees. The employer, therefore, should insist on communicating the situation to the union.

If a settlement is reached, then it is very important to have a comprehensive release signed by the complainant. The release should include the employee's acknowledgment that the settlement is intended to be full and final, and that it is intended to settle any claims that the employee has or could have under human rights legislation. Although employees cannot contract out of human rights legislation, a release of past acts of alleged harassment that settle an actual or potential human rights complaint should be valid. A human rights complaint filed after the employee signed a valid and enforceable release that specifically releases the employer from liability associated with a harassment complaint that existed at the time of signing, should be dismissed on a preliminary basis on the grounds of bad faith.[9] In the case of a unionized employee, it will be necessary to have the union review the release and to sign off on any terms of settlement.

6.b.   Authorized Leaves Of Absence or Changes in Duties

In most cases, the complainant will feel unable to continue working under the same conditions that triggered the complaint while the matter is investigated and resolved. The complainant, however, may be able to continue working in a different capacity or subject to other changes that provide some protection or peace of mind. If so, during the investigation, the employer should take steps to protect the complainant's safety and emotional well-being. In effect, much like dealing with an employee who is partially disabled, the employer should attempt to accommodate the complainant while it evaluates the complaint. Depending on the nature of the allegations, the accommodation may involve changing the location of the complainant's work station to separate the complainant from the alleged harasser, changing the complainant's reporting relationships or work schedule, assigning tasks for the complainant to complete at home or granting the complainant time off work, until the matter is resolved.

If the only suitable accommodation is granting the complainant time off work, the employer is well advised to continue the complainant's compen-

---

[9]   *Chow v. Mobil Oil Canada Ltd.*, [1999] 12 W.W.R. 373 (Alta. Q.B.) and *Pritchard v. Ontario (Human Rights Commission)* (1999), 45 O.R. (3d) 97 (Ont. Div. Ct.).

sation and benefits until the matter is resolved. If the complaint does not pass the four preliminary tests, the matter may be resolved in a matter of hours or days. However, if the employer determines that a formal investigation is required, the investigation could take a number of weeks. During this period, whether hours, days or weeks, the complainant's status is that of an authorized leave of absence with pay. The employer should keep the complainant apprised of the status of the matter and should continue to look for opportunities to return the complainant to suitable alternative work.

6.c.   Workers' Compensation Benefits

In extreme situations, the complainant may claim to have suffered mental distress and be incapable of working for medical reasons, as a result of the workplace harassment. In this situation, if the employee is covered by workplace safety and insurance or workers' compensation legislation, the employer may be required to complete the appropriate forms within the requisite time limits to notify the appropriate agency of a potential claim. Generally, it is very difficult for a complainant to establish a claim for workers' compensation benefits for mental distress arising out of workplace harassment, except in cases of severe cases such as sexual assault. In Ontario, for example, benefits for mental stress are limited to "an acute reaction to a sudden and unexpected traumatic event arising out of an in the course of employment."[10] To assess the obligation to report an unauthorized employee absence following a complaint, employers should seek external, professional advice.

6.d.   Disability Benefits

Where a complainant claims to be incapable of working as a result of the mental distress attributable to the alleged harassment, the complainant may be eligible to apply for sick benefits through a company disability program or through Employment Insurance. The complainant's eligibility for such benefits will be subject to the terms and conditions of the benefit plans, and dependent on providing satisfactory medical evidence of his or her condition. A claim for disability coverage, if accepted, would be instead of, and not in addition to, any claim for workers' compensation coverage.

---

[10]   *Workplace Safety and Insurance Act, 1997*, S.O. 1997, c. 16, Sch. A, s. 13(5).

7. The Employment Status of the Accused Upon Receipt of the Complaint

It is important to remember that the person accused of engaging in harassing conduct should be treated as innocent until proven guilty. As indicated in Section 5 above, the employer must take care not to compromise any action that may be required of police authorities and, in particular, not to threaten the accused in any fashion in exchange for resolving either the complaint or an ongoing employment situation.

In light of the presumption of innocence, in most situations, there should be no changes to the work conditions of the accused, while the employer evaluates the complaint. However, in situations where the allegations are so grave as to cause the employer concern for the safety of the complainant or other employees, including the alleged aggressor, it may be necessary to remove the accused from the workplace, pending the resolution of the matter. If the accused is relieved of his or her employment duties pending the evaluation of the matter, the employer should continue his or her compensation and benefits. During this period, the status of the accused status is that of an authorized leave of absence with pay.

The exception to a leave with pay would be if it is readily apparent from the outset that there has been some misconduct and the only real issue is the severity of the misconduct and the consequence that should follow. Note that this determination should not be made based on a complainant's allegations alone—corroboration is required. In such cases, a leave of absence without pay pending the conclusion of the investigation would be more appropriate.

Relieving the accused of his or her duties pending the evaluation of the matter involves a degree of risk and liability exposure to the employer. In removing the accused's employment duties, there is some risk that the employee will allege that to have been constructively dismissed, and therefore sue for damages for wrongful dismissal. To minimize such risk, the employer should reassure the accused that the measure is merely preventative and temporary, that no conclusions have been made regarding the allegations, that an opportunity to respond to the allegations will be provided, and that a decision has not been made to terminate the employment relationship. The employer should keep the accused regularly informed of the status of the matter, while he or she is off work.

Although there is the risk of a claim of constructive dismissal, there are three practical points to be made. First, modern courts are very sympathetic to the responsibility of an employer to be both diligent and careful in the face of a complaint of workplace harassment. Second, by the time the matter gets to court, it will likely be much clearer on the facts. If the accused is exonerated, then it is likely that some reconciliation will have been effected; otherwise, the case may involve a dismissal for cause, not just a constructive dismissal. Finally, if the leave is with pay, then, so long as the leave continues, there are no damages. Once the investigation concludes, if the accused is exonerated, then a court may well conclude that the accused should mitigate any loss by simply returning to active employment.

In considering whether to keep the accused at the worksite, the employer must balance the risks associated with keeping him or her on-site against the risks associated with temporarily relieving the accused from his or her employment duties. In striking this balance, although the risk cannot be entirely dismissed, it is our view that little weight should be given to the risk of an eventual claim of constructive dismissal.

◆
CHAPTER 5

HOW TO SELECT THE INVESTIGATOR

1. The Importance of Selecting the Appropriate Investigator

Assuming that the complaint has passed the four-part preliminary test set out in Chapter 4, the employer must commence a formal investigation into the allegations of harassment promptly. The first step is to select an investigator to carry out the investigation. In some situations, it may be appropriate to have an investigative team of more than one investigator, so long as the investigative model does not become unwieldy. Selecting the appropriate investigator is critical to ensuring that the employer obtains the necessary information with which it can make an informed decision on how to respond to the harassment allegations.

The investigator will be responsible for meeting with the individuals involved, obtaining all of the necessary information, making assessments as to credibility and reporting back to the employer. If the individuals who meet with the investigator are uncomfortable providing the necessary information or if the investigation is carried-out improperly, the investigation will be flawed and counter-productive. A poorly run investigation can expose an employer to further liability and unnecessary costs.[1]

2. The Investigator's Background

It is very important that the investigator understand human rights legislation and the concept of harassment in particular. This will ensure that the investigation is conducted and the questions are asked in a manner that accords with statutory requirements. The investigator should also have experience and sensitivity in dealing with employees and employment issues.

The perception of neutrality and a lack of bias to both the complainant and the alleged harasser are key qualities the investigator must possess. Therefore, the person chosen should not be in a position of influence over these individuals, and should not make decisions regarding their compensation, discipline, discharge, demotion, opportunities for advancement, or any other terms or conditions of their employment.

Care should be taken to select an investigator to suit the situation. For example, if the complaint is one of sexual harassment and the allegations warrant it, the employer should consider having both a man and a woman conduct the investigation. This will ensure a gender-balanced investigation. Similarly, if the complaint involves harassment based on race or religion, having a person from a similar background, who can offer insight into the meaning of events and comments, conduct the investigation may be preferable.

3. Internal Versus External Investigators

3.a.   General

In deciding whether or not to use an internal or external investigator, employers should consider the nature of the allegations, against whom the allegations are made, the availability of an appropriate and impartial internal investigator, the role of legal counsel, and the costs of and preference for retaining an external investigator or using internal resources.

---

[1]   See *OPSEU (Hurge) v. Ontario (Ministry of the Attorney General)* (1995), unrep. GSB no. 348/92 (Kaplan), in which a 22-day hearing took place over two years, into disciplinary action taken by the employer following a sexual harassment investigation. The panel of the Crown Employees Grievance Settlement Board determined that, although the disciplinary action was appropriate, the investigation was flawed, and that the report should be removed from the grievor's file.

Often times, in medium- to large-sized employers, employees in human resources will have the appropriate background and experience to conduct an investigation. However, as discussed below, there may be instances where an internal investigator would not be appropriate, even if there is an employee who would be capable of handling the investigation.

In more detail, here are the five factors that should guide an employer in deciding whether or not to use an internal or external investigator:

3.b.   Nature and Severity of the Allegations

First, employers should consider the nature and severity of the allegations. Sexual harassment investigations are usually difficult because of the sensitivity of the allegations, especially if the family of the accused or the victim may be affected in a significant way by the results of the investigation. These tense situations are often made more difficult, as the events in issue frequently occur in private, away from the public eye, without any witnesses or material evidence. In those situations, typically referred to as "he said/she said" cases, issues of credibility will likely be the deciding factors. Credibility does not turn on gut instinct; it requires the analysis of an experienced investigator, which may be beyond the capability of even an employee who is well-versed in human rights law. In any event, if the allegations are serious with a high liability exposure, retaining an external investigator would demonstrate that the employer handled the situation with due diligence.

3.c.   Identity of the Accused

An employer's decision to use an internal or external investigator may depend on the identity of the person against whom the allegations of harassment are made. If the allegations are made against or involve the employees who normally would be responsible for conducting the investigation, or if the allegations involve a senior member of management, an external investigator should be retained.

Further, it would be inappropriate for an internal employee to conduct an investigation into allegations against a superior who has the ability to affect the employee's terms and conditions of work. Understandably, in such instances, there would be considerable pressure on the investigator, in fact or in perception, to arrive at a conclusion that does not negatively affect the alleged harasser.

Also, where the allegations are of widespread harassment against a number of employees, it may be appropriate to use an external investigator. In those instances, there may be too much internal pressure on an internal investigator to be able to conduct an impartial investigation. In any event, the workload involved in carrying out an investigation with a number of employees who may be affected would be considerable, as would be the pressure on an investigator who may be faced with significantly impacting several careers. This kind of strain, both in terms of the work involved and the potential consequences, may be much easier for an "outsider" to handle.

Where the allegations are made by or against a third party, an external investigator may be necessary. For example, if the allegations are made by or against a customer, the use of a neutral, external investigator will strengthen the perception that the employer is conducting a fair and unbiased investigation, and is taking the allegations seriously.

3.d.   Availability of Internal, Impartial, Knowledgeable Investigator

An employer should retain an external investigator if there are no employees available internally with the requisite impartiality and knowledge that is required to conduct an investigation. It is also important for the investigator to have the time available to complete an investigation in an expeditious fashion. If the potential internal investigator cannot be relieved of other duties in order to focus on the investigation, an external investigator would be more appropriate. As stated by one adjudicator, "Not only is this a matter of fairness, but it will also demonstrate to workers and managers alike that the parties' shared commitment to ensuring a sexual-harassment-free workplace is being taken seriously, evidenced, as it were, by directing sufficient resources towards ensuring the timely investigation of sexual harassment complaints."[2] If the employer lacks the necessary internal resources, even the question of whether or not to conduct an investigation at all would benefit from the advice of an outside expert.

3.e.   The Role of Legal Counsel

The employer should consider the role, if any, that legal counsel will play in the investigation. Sometimes employers attempt to cloak the investigation or the investigation report in solicitor-client privilege, so that the in-

---

[2]   *Supra*, note 81 at 168.

formation obtained during the investigation will not have to be disclosed in any subsequent legal proceeding. The only chance you have of attaching such privilege to an investigation is to use a lawyer. Only in limited circumstances would privilege attach on the basis that the dominant purpose of the investigation and the resulting report is litigation.[3]

There are a number of other ways that legal counsel can assist with the investigation. Experienced employment lawyers well-versed in human rights law are capable of conducting or coordinating an expert investigation. As such, the employer may decide to retain a lawyer to be the investigator and prepare the investigation report. As a note of caution, where a lawyer acts as the investigator, he or she may become a witness to any subsequent legal proceeding and may be unable to represent the employer in any subsequent legal proceedings involving this matter.

Another option is to retain a lawyer to coordinate or oversee the investigation. As such, the lawyer would retain the investigator, who would report back to the lawyer. Based on the factual findings of the investigator, the lawyer would report back to the employer and assist in the decisions about what should be done as a result of the investigation. Depending on the arrangement, the investigator would be expected to draft the factual findings in the investigation report, either as part of the report or in a separate document. The lawyer would set out the relevant law, would draw conclusions in applying the facts to the law, and would therefore make recommendations for action.

Even if not to oversee the investigation, a lawyer may be retained to draft the investigation report, or at least the part of the report that deals with the law, and recommendations arising from the application of the investigation facts to the law. Either as the expert who oversees the investigation, or as the expert who provides an opinion to the organization based on the investigation facts, the lawyer should not be compellable as a witness to the proceedings. As such, the lawyer should be able to continue representing the employer in any subsequent legal proceedings. If it is important for the employer to continue to use the lawyer as counsel in any legal proceedings arising from the investigation, the best practice is to have the investigator prepare a factual report and to have the lawyer prepare a separate document in the nature of an opinion that would draw conclusions and make recommendations.

---

[3]   There must be more than a possibility of litigation arising from the complaint for the claim of litigation privilege to attach; the litigation must be a pending or definite prospect. See *Lattanzio v. Jones* (1989), 33 C.P.C. (2d) 160 (Ont. Dist. Ct.).

3.f.　　Preference and Costs

Some employers simply prefer to use an external investigator to avoid any potential allegations of bias or unfairness, and to ensure that the investigation is properly conducted. An external investigator may be able to provide valuable feedback on all matters learned in the investigation process, regardless if the conduct is found to constitute prohibited harassment. In other words, any good investigation should deal not only with the priority of the specific complaint, but should also involve lessons of general application that will benefit the employer as it goes forward.

There are costs associated with conducting a harassment investigation, regardless of whether or not an internal or external investigator is used. The costs of an external investigator are more apparent on their face, but there are significant hidden costs associated with an internal investigator. The investigator will lose the time required to perform his or her regular duties while conducting the investigation. Also, an internal investigator may be less efficient and less organized. As a result, more time from the witnesses may be required to conduct the interviews and to ask follow-up questions. Further, an internal investigator may take longer to prepare the investigation report, as a result of trying to balance other duties, thereby causing a delay in providing a response to the complainant. Finally, and perhaps most important of all, an investigation into allegations of workplace harassment creates ongoing ripples throughout the workplace, such that the dynamic of internal relationships may be forever altered in a way that has long-term negative effects for the employer. This ripple effect will happen whether the investigator is external or internal, but it is more likely, and likely to be more severe, with an internal investigation. In particular, the internal investigator may be permanently and negatively impacted in terms of his or her operational effectiveness.

♦

CHAPTER 6

HOW TO CONDUCT THE INTERVIEWS

1. General

The procedure used for conducting the interviews into allegations of harassment will vary depending on each situation. Nonetheless, the following are general guidelines for conducting such interviews that should be adapted to meet the needs of the situation.

The same investigator should conduct all of the interviews during the investigation, if possible. If two or three investigators are used, they should all be present at all interviews, or at least the key interviews. This will ensure consistency in the investigation and provide one person with a complete understanding of the situation. If there are numerous witnesses to be interviewed and more than one investigator assigned, investigators may have to split up, at least with the "minor" witnesses, to ensure that the investigation is completed in a timely and efficient, yet effective manner.

2. Where and When to Conduct the Interviews

Generally, interviews are conducted in a private meeting room in the workplace, during working hours. The workplace is normally a convenient location for the witnesses, and one with which the witnesses are comfortable and familiar. However, if there are concerns about confidentiality or safety, and particularly the safety of the complainant, the interviews should be conducted off-site. In addition, if the complainant requests a location other than the workplace, and if the request has a reasonable basis, the employer should grant the request.

3. The Presence of a Witness During the Interviews

There are times when a witness should be present during the interviews, at the direction of the employer. We will use the term "investigator's witness" to avoid confusion between the witness being interviewed and the individual attending on the investigator's behalf or at the direction of the employer. An investigator's witness is useful to confirm the investigator's version of the interview, especially if there is any concern that the person being interviewed might attack the credibility of the investigator or the fairness of the procedure. These concerns are most prevalent when an internal investigator conducts the interviews. Accordingly, such "sensitive" or potentially difficult interviews should be conducted in the presence of an investigator's witness.

These concerns also may arise in particularly sensitive interviews that are conducted by an external investigator. For example, where a complainant has alleged that no one is treating him or her fairly on the basis of one of the prohibited grounds of harassment, the complainant may also view any external investigator hired and paid for by the employer as incapable of treating him or her fairly. Having an investigator's witness present will protect and confirm the integrity and objectivity of the investigation.

Some employers will want an investigator's witness present if the investigation is conducted by an external investigator for at least two other reasons. First, the employer will want to satisfy itself that the external investigator is proceeding in an appropriate and measured fashion. Second, these are very important learning experiences for an employer, whatever the result. The employer cannot change the fact that a complaint has been made. In dealing with that complaint effectively, the employer can improve its chances of avoiding similar complaints or properly responding to complaints internally in the future. It is not unusual, for example, for an employer facing a serious harassment complaint, to retain an external investigator to work with an internal employee who, as a training exercise, will shadow the investigation and attend the interviews.

Any investigator's witness who attends interviews should be someone who is neutral and not in a position to affect the terms and conditions of employment of the witness being interviewed. The investigator's witness present for the interviews does not have to be the same person throughout all of the interviews, but it is best to either have the same person or at least to limit the number of different investigator's witnesses who are used, to preserve the confidentiality and integrity of the investigation.

The role of the investigator's witness is to take notes during the interview. The investigator's witness should not speak during the interview, as this will disrupt the flow of conversation, and may create a perception of unfairness. The point is to have two witnesses: the person being interviewed and the investigator's witness and one investigator, not two investigators "against" one witness. Any investigator's witness who is used in the investigation may be called as a witness in a subsequent legal proceeding arising from the complaint.

4. Preparing for the Interviews

4.a. Transcribing the Interviews

The investigator or the investigator's witness, where applicable, should take notes during the interview, as this is the best means of capturing the full discussion. At the outset of the interview, the investigator should advise the person being interviewed that notes will be made. The investigator should pace the interview so that full answers can be recorded. The notes should be reviewed as soon as possible after the interview to ensure they are complete, accurate and logical. Any additions or revisions should be made at that time. Ideally, notes are taken either by hand or typed on a computer so that they are reviewed, corrected and signed by the person being interviewed before he or she leaves the interview.

To the extent possible, the notes should reiterate the questions asked and the answers given, and note any observations during the interview, not just summarize what transpired. To this end, a list of questions generally should be prepared in advance to ensure that at least the questions on the list have been asked and answered. This list of questions, however, should not limit the interview. The interviewer must listen carefully to the answer to each question posed, and follow up such answer with any relevant questions that flow from it. While an interview may be scripted in part in advance, it is incumbent upon the interviewer to deviate from the script whenever appropriate.

The notes should not include any personal opinions, comments or judgments. Because different people will reach different conclusions on reviewing the same facts, it is important that no "judgment calls" be made or opinions formed during the course of the investigation, and certainly not in the middle of any particular interview. Reaching conclusions or forming opinions before all of the witnesses have been interviewed may create a perception of bias and unfairness. Naturally, there is an organic nature to all of this; each answer given will have an impact on subsequent questions that are asked and other witnesses who may have to participate in the investigation. The key is to retain an open mind until the investigation has been completed.

As has been discussed earlier, it is important to remember that the complainant may pursue the complaint beyond the internal process and file a complaint with external authorities. If that occurs, the notes taken during the investigation may become evidence in any future proceedings. For this reason, it is particularly important that the interview notes are accurate and objective, without any subjective analysis or comments.

Although a tape recorder may provide the most accurate record of an interview, it is not recommended because a tape recorder can make people nervous and reluctant to speak openly. If a tape recorder is used, it must be openly communicated to the person being interviewed and a transcript should be prepared as soon as possible following the interview for review by all participants, including the witness.

As we will discuss below, whether or not a tape recorder is used, any records that are made during an interview should be reviewed promptly by the employee who was the subject of the interview, and signed as accurate records of the questions and answers during the interview. This is the creation of witness statements that could be evidentiary and, at least, could be used to control a witness who is contradictory in a subsequent legal proceeding.

4.b. Disclosing Details of the Complaint

There should be considerable discussion in advance of the interviews as to the extent to which it is appropriate to reveal any details of the complaint. The accused has confidentiality rights and expectations, as does the complainant. Unless it is obvious that the witness is familiar with the allegations, the investigator should be careful to provide only the information that is necessary to conduct a meaningful interview. In many cases, especially using an expert investigator, this can be done without revealing the identity of the persons involved in the alleged incident or incidents. This is a very important point that has to be carefully considered in advance of the investigation and handled carefully during each interview. Allegations alone can be very harmful to a person's employment, both the complainant and the accused, regardless of the ultimate conclusions that are reached.

5. Procedural Guidelines for Effective Interviews

The section above has set up a framework for conducting interviews. The preceding chapter has dealt with who will lead the investigation. The following sub-sections are intended to provide a guideline for each interview that is conducted during the course of the investigation, starting with the sequence of the interviews, and then a standard process for each interview.

5.a. The Sequence of the Interviews

To get the basic story from the outset, and to ensure that the accused has every reasonable opportunity to provide responses and explanations, we suggest the following standard sequence for conducting interviews. Note that the interview of the complainant is separate and apart from whatever meeting took place when the complaint was first made. Here is the recommended order for the interviews, first to last:

- The complainant;
- The witnesses suggested by the complainant;
- The accused;
- The witnesses suggested by the accused, if any;
- Follow-up meetings to obtain clarification on any issues, or to put any allegations of the accused to the complainant; and

- A final follow-up meeting with the accused if any outstanding issues have arisen following the initial meeting with the accused that require comment or explanation.

5.b.   Commencing the Interviews

The investigator should adhere to the following protocol at the start of each of the interviews:

- The investigator should explain that he or she has been asked by the employer to conduct an investigation as a result of its receipt of a complaint of harassment in the workplace.
- The investigator should reveal those details of the complaint necessary to conduct a meaningful interview.
- The investigator should advise the person being interviewed of his or her educational background and experience to establish credibility and authority for conducting the investigation. The investigator should provide a business card and contact information.
- The investigator should explain his or her role, and the role of the investigator's witness, who is present, if any. The investigator should state that the investigator's witness, if any, is present to take notes, as it is difficult for the investigator to listen and take proper notes. The investigator should confirm that the person being interviewed will have the opportunity to review those notes and, where appropriate, that the witness will be asked to sign a witness statement at the end of the interview. The investigator should clarify that the investigator's witness will not ask any questions or participate in the interview, except to take notes.
- The investigator should explain that the investigation process is confidential, but limited disclosure may be required in order to conduct the investigation.
- As well, the investigator should make it clear that there is the possibility of a legal proceeding at some point following the investigation, at which the person being interviewed may be called as a witness. The investigator should make clear that he or she is not responsible for that proceeding and cannot make any promises or predictions as to whether the person being interviewed would have to testify.
- The investigator should explain that the person being interviewed must keep the information discussed during their meeting confidential, which means that he or she cannot discuss it with anyone else, neither an employee nor a friend, nor a family member. This need for confidentiality should be very clearly stressed.

- The investigator should advise the person being interviewed that if he or she has any follow-up information recalled after the interview, including any corrections or clarifications, or any subsequent questions, he or she should contact the investigator without delay.
- The investigator should advise the person being interviewed that there will be an investigation report provided to the employer at the completion of the investigation and that appropriate action following the investigation depends on complete and accurate answers to questions asked throughout the investigation.

5.c.   Conduct During the Interviews

The investigator should adhere to the following protocol during the interviews:

- Avoid interrupting the people being interviewed. The exception to this is if the person is clearly off topic and not responsive. However, there should be considerable leeway as this is an information gathering exercise and not a cross-examination.
- For each allegation, encourage the person being interviewed to describe his or her version of the events without any questions, other than prompts like "what happened next". Leading questions that suggest the answer should be avoided. Once the narrative has been completed for each allegation, go back to the start of the story and ask any questions.
- Clarify any inconsistencies. If the person being interviewed gives inconsistent answers, bring it to his or her attention and ask for an explanation for why the information provided was inconsistent.
- Focus the person being interviewed on providing information that he or she knows "first hand", not what the person heard about from other people. Reiterating what a person heard about from someone else is called "hearsay". Hearsay is not given much weight in hearings, and should not be given much weight in the investigation.

5.d.   Conduct at the Conclusion of the Interviews

The investigator should abide by the following protocol at the end of each interview:

- The investigator should ask if there is anything else the person would like to add to the discussion.
- The investigator should remind the person to contact the investigator with any additional information he or she remembers after the interview.

- The investigator should remind the person to keep the interview confidential.
- The investigator should let the person know that the investigator may have additional questions once the interview notes are reviewed, and this may require some follow-up questions.
- The investigator should advise that the employer will not tolerate any interference with its investigation or reprisals of any kind. The investigator should make himself or herself available as a contact person to whom any reprisals or concerns about the integrity of the investigation should be reported.
- If the interview notes of the investigator or the investigator's witness are legible, the investigator should ask the person who was interviewed to review them, make any changes, and sign a statement agreeing to their accuracy. Wherever possible, this should be completed before the interview concludes. If these notes need to be typed, the investigator may follow-up afterwards with the typed version to have the witness sign off on them. Whether this is necessary will depend on the severity of the allegations and the budget for and the nature of the investigation. If the person who was interviewed refuses to sign the notes as a confirmation of their accuracy, then a note to that effect should be written.
- The investigator should thank the person for participating in the process.

6. Interviewing the Complainant

6.a. General

Complainants tend to provide only vague allegations of harassment, without sufficient details to enable the employer to conduct an investigation. When this occurs, it is usually necessary to follow-up with the complainant to get a better understanding of the allegations.

Whether or not this is the case, the first person the investigator should meet with is the complainant. The investigator should explain that the employer is taking the allegations seriously, and that more information is required in order to do a complete investigation.

The investigator must explain that he or she may be meeting with the accused and any witnesses to find out their understanding of the allegations. The investigator should provide the complainant with the timeframe for when he or she expects to follow-up with the complainant with any additional questions that may have arisen during the investigation, and the timeframe for reporting back with the outcome of the investigation.

6.b.   Obtaining the Complainant's Version

Once the investigator completes his or her introduction and explanations, he or she should ask the complainant to provide all of the details of the allegations in his or her own words. The investigator should allow the complainant to go through the entire story from start to finish without interruption. Only after the complainant has completed his or her version of the events, should the investigator start back at the beginning with questions to elicit information the complainant may have left out.

6.c.   Asking the Seven "W" Questions

With respect to each allegation raised by the complainant, the investigator should try to obtain the following information, referred to as the seven "W" questions. That is, "who" said or did "what" to "whom", "where", "when", "why" and what "witnesses" were present:

Here is a useful check-list.

- **Who**—who said or did the alleged conduct.
- **What**—what was said or done.
- **Whom**—to whom was it said or done.
- **Where**—where did the incident occur (e.g.: whose office, where in the lunch room); use photographs or diagrams to get a clear picture of the scene.
- **When**—when did the incident occur (date and time).
- **Why**—why did the incident occur (what happened just before and after, was there a pre-existing history, including past incidents).
- **Witnesses**—what witnesses saw the incident; what did the witness say or do.

For the purposes of a complete investigation, each of the "W's" on the above list should be checked off. The only items about which there may be little information will be the last two. It may not be apparent why the incident happened, and the incident may be an isolated situation. As for witnesses, it is often the case that there are no witnesses to the incident itself, although there may be witnesses who are able to comment on prior history and aftermath.

6.d. Events Occurring Before and After the Incident

To get a better understanding of "why" something occurred, the investigator should ask what happened immediately *before* and *after* the alleged incident. Asking what happened just before the alleged incident will enable the investigator to find out what, if anything, triggered it. Asking what happened just after the alleged incident will enable the investigator to find out how the complainant responded to the incident at the time it occurred. If the complainant is reacting differently to the alleged incident after the passage of time than he or she did at the time it occurred, this might provide some insight into the complainant's credibility or motive for subsequently reporting the incident.

7. Trivial, Frivolous, Vexatious or Bad Faith Complaints

After interviewing the complainant, the investigator may be concerned that the allegations, even if accepted as true, are trivial, frivolous, vexatious, or made in bad faith. If this arises, the investigator should advise the senior company official to whom he or she is reporting.

At this juncture, a decision should be made on whether to continue with the investigation. If a decision is made not to proceed with the investigation, the complainant will have to be informed of the decision. Remember that this conclusion can be reached only in unusual cases. Further, the employer should consider other methods of dealing with the issues raised in the complaint. This may include a meeting with the complainant and the accused to discuss the issues. There may also be a basis for imposing discipline on the complainant if the complaint was filed in bad faith.

8. Interviewing Witnesses

The witnesses named by the complainant, if any, would generally be interviewed after the complainant. Similarly, the witnesses named by the accused would generally be interviewed after the accused. The investigator will need to determine which witnesses, if any, should be interviewed. The more witnesses that are interviewed, the greater the confidentiality of the investigation is compromised. The complainant and accused may provide the names of a number of witnesses to each incident, but that does not mean that all of those witnesses have to be interviewed.

Generally, if both the complainant and accused have named the same witness, that witness should be interviewed. If there are witnesses to the more significant incidents, the investigator may decide to only interview them and not the witnesses to the more trivial incidents.

Sometimes the complainant or accused will provide names of people they want the investigator to interview, even though those people have no "first hand" knowledge of the incidents in issue. For example, the complainant who went home and told her family about the incidents at work may want the investigator to interview the family members to confirm what she told them. Or, the accused may want the investigator to interview his or her family or friends, so they can say what a great person the accused is, and how the accused would never engage in the conduct for which he or she has been accused. Generally, the investigator should not conduct such interviews. These interviews would provide only hearsay evidence, which as previously discussed, holds little weight.

In ordering the interviews with the witnesses, the investigator should start with the witness who will likely have the most information, or information on the most serious incidents, then work down the list to those with the least information, or information on the least serious incidents. If the investigator learns enough information from the most important witnesses, he or she may decide it is unnecessary to continue interviewing additional witnesses.

If the witnesses are employees who will be present on the worksite, it is unnecessary for them to be advised in advance that they will be interviewed. However, if the witness does not regularly attend the worksite, it may be necessary to schedule the meeting with the witness in advance. Generally, it is unnecessary to explain the reason for the interview beforehand.

9. Interviewing the Accused

The objectives in meeting with the accused are to provide him or her with an opportunity to respond to the allegations that have been made, and to obtain his or her version of the events. As such, the accused must be presented with the allegations that have been made against him or her in sufficient detail, so that he or she can fully respond to them.

In presenting the allegations to the accused, the investigator must be careful to reiterate only the facts, without characterizing the allegations. For example, the investigator should state: "The complainant said that last Monday, you said the following to her ..." The investigator should not state: "You have been accused of sexual harassment."

The investigator may give a copy of the complaint to the accused or a list of the key allegations, but this is not required. The investigator may prefer to simply read aloud each allegation and give the accused the opportunity to respond to each.

With respect to each allegation, the investigator should follow the same procedure, as with the complainant, namely, the accused should tell his version of the incident from start to finish, without interruptions. Once completed, the investigator should start back at the beginning of the story with any questions. The investigator should try to obtain the answers of the accused for the seven "W" questions, that is, "who" said "what" to "whom", "where", "when", "why", and what "witnesses" were present.

Sometimes the accused will want to have a lawyer present. As this is an internal investigation, technically there is no obligation on the employer to provide or allow outside legal counsel. Even so, there may be circumstances in which the presence of legal counsel is not objectionable, subject to agreement as to the limited role the lawyer would play during interview. Allowing the presence of the accused's legal counsel will, for example, avoid an allegation of bad faith or unfair dealing to be raised at a later date against the employer. It also may eliminate the ability of the accused's legal counsel to continue to represent the accused in any subsequent legal proceeding since the lawyer cannot serve both as witness and advocate. If the accused is a unionized employee, he or she may have the right to have a union steward present, depending on what is set out in the collective agreement. It is of critical importance to comply with any rights or procedures set out in the collective agreement. The failure to do so may nullify any discipline that may be imposed.

The accused should be cautioned about speaking with anyone about the allegations, especially the complainant, or in any way interfering with the investigation.

10. Uncooperative Participants

In most investigations into employee misconduct, the employer should rightfully expect a high degree of cooperation from its own employees. If an incident occurred during working hours and if the investigation interview is taking place during working hours, then there is, generally, no legitimate basis for the employee who is being interviewed to refuse to answer all reasonable inquiries of the investigator. However, that being said, it is important to be sensitive to the special tensions that are inherent in a situation of alleged workplace harassment. In the result, the employer's response to a participant's failure to cooperate likely will depend on who is refusing to cooperate.

10.a. Uncooperative Complainant

If the complainant refuses to cooperate, he or she should be given the option of withdrawing the complaint. If the complainant decides to withdraw the complaint, ask the complainant to confirm the withdrawal in writing. If the complainant does not confirm the withdrawal in writing, the employer should write a letter to the complainant confirming the withdrawal of the complaint.

A complainant can withdraw a complaint at any time during the investigation process. It is important to understand that the withdrawal of the complaint does not determine whether or not the employer has obligations under human rights legislation that may have been breached. Therefore, the fact that the complaint is withdrawn may not alleviate the employer's obligations to investigate the allegations. Depending on the status of the investigation at the time of the withdrawal of the complaint, the employer may or may not have sufficient information upon which it can continue the investigation. If the employer has sufficient information, it should continue the investigation. If the employer lacks sufficient information, the complainant should be advised that without his or her continued participation, the employer will have no choice but to dismiss the complaint. If this occurs, the employer should confirm in writing to the complainant the reason for the dismissal of the complaint.

10.b. Uncooperative Accused

The employer must inform the accused of the allegations against him or her. If the accused refuses to cooperate in the investigation and respond to the allegations, the employer should notify the accused that without his or her cooperation, it will have only the complainant's and the complainant's witnesses' version of events. The employer should advise the accused that it will be making decisions based on the information and evidence that it has. The employer should warn the accused that he or she may be subject to discipline up to and including dismissal, depending on the outcome of the investigation. Due to the serious implications that flow from the accused's uncooperativeness, the employer should send a letter to the accused confirming his or her refusal to cooperate in the investigation and the potential consequences of such refusal.

10.c. Uncooperative Witnesses

While a witness who is a co-worker may have no valid reason for refusing to answer an investigator's questions in the context of a workplace harassment investigation, witnesses may be concerned that they will be subject to reprisals from either the complainant or the accused. Fear of reprisal may certainly affect an employee's willingness to be involved or to be open and forthright in an investigation interview. If the witness reports directly to either the complainant or the accused and that person has the ability to affect their terms and conditions of employment, a certain amount of reluctance is understandable. The investigator should advise all witnesses that their full cooperation is expected and important in order for a thorough investigation to be conducted and appropriate action taken. Although each situation must be assessed on a case-by-case basis, it is generally difficult to discipline uncooperative witnesses for their refusal to disclose the full extent of their knowledge to an investigator in a workplace harassment investigation.

11. Liability for Statements Made During the Interviews

Sometimes people being interviewed are concerned about giving evidence in an investigation, out of fear that they will be sued for defamation. However, it has been recognized that the information obtained in conducting a human rights investigation, generally, cannot be the subject of a defamation lawsuit because it is privileged.

In the case of *Ayangma v. NAV Canada*[1], when Mr. Ayangma was not offered a position as an air traffic controller with Transport Canada, he filed a complaint with the Canadian Human Rights Commission alleging that he had been discriminated against in his employment. In conducting the investigation, one of the panel members that interviewed Mr. Ayangma told the Commission's investigator that Mr. Ayangma may have had access to the written test, which explained his high score on the written test and poor score on the oral test.

---

[1] *Ayangma v. NAV Canada* (2001), 203 D.L.R. (4th) 717 (P.E.I. C.A.), application for leave to appeal dismissed (2001), [2001] S.C.C.A. No. 76, 2001 CarswellPEI 129 (S.C.C.), reconsideration refused (2002), 2002 CarswellPEI 96 (S.C.C.).

Mr. Ayangma obtained a copy of the Commission's investigation file under the *Access to Information Act*. Upon learning of the panel member's comments, Mr. Ayangma sued the panel member for defamation. The Court said that the comment made by the panel member was protected by the principle of absolute privilege and, as such it could not be the basis for the defamation lawsuit. Accordingly, the Court dismissed the lawsuit.

♦

CHAPTER 7

HOW TO WRITE THE INVESTIGATION REPORT

1. Overview

In writing an investigation report, it is important to remember that in addition to filing an internal complaint with the employer, the complainant may seek further recourse. As discussed earlier in Section 5 of Chapter 1, for unionized employees, this might include filing a grievance under a collective agreement, which if unresolved in the grievance procedure, may eventually proceed to an arbitration hearing. Further, a non-unionized employee may file a human rights complaint with the governing human rights commission, or commence a lawsuit in court. As such, the investigation report may become evidence in external legal proceedings. With this in mind, it is important that the investigation report be properly drafted.

It is recommended that the facts learned from the investigation be kept separate from the conclusions and opinions reached as a result of those facts. This way, the investigation report dealing with the facts will reflect a neutral, objective investigation. Also, as different decision-makers may reach different conclusions based on the same facts, a neutral, objective report will enable readers to reach their own conclusions. Accordingly, it is recommended that two reports be prepared. This may also assist in admitting or excluding parts of the reports as evidence in any subsequent legal proceedings.

The format of the reports may vary depending on the depth of the investigation, the number of allegations addressed, and the number of witnesses interviewed. Nonetheless, the content of the reports should adhere to the following guidelines.

2. The First Report: Stating the Facts, Evidence and Observations

The first report should contain the facts and observations obtained by reviewing the complaint and conducting the interviews. This should be an objective summary of the allegations and the evidence. This report should describe each allegation, followed by the response of the accused to the allegation, and the comments from each witness. If someone being interviewed gave inconsistent answers during the interview, the inconsistencies should be identified in the report. The report also should include any specific or general observations noted during the investigation, such as:

- The accused began shouting and his face turned red when the investigator asked this particular question.
- The complainant cried when discussing this allegation.
- Overall, the complainant gave his evidence in a clear, straight-forward and consistent manner, without hesitating; whereas, the accused appeared nervous, was shaking his pen, did not look the investigator in the eye, and gave inconsistent answers.

In other words, the report should set out the objective factual observations that will underlie the investigator's credibility findings.

If either the complainant or the accused pursue legal action arising out of the internal complaint or the results of the investigation, it is likely that this first report will be admitted as evidence in that proceeding.

3. The Second Report: Stating the Opinions, Conclusions and Recommendations

Wherever allegations continue to be disputed at the conclusion of the investigation, the second report should set out the investigator's opinion as to the credibility of the witnesses, including the complainant and the accused, based on the evidence received and the demeanour in which it was provided. The investigator will be in the best position to assess credibility and, particularly in a "he said/she said" complaint, the investigator's assessment will be critical.

The second report should contain the investigator's findings drawn from the facts and legal analysis, if any, that has been applied. If a lawyer has been retained by the employer to provide the legal analysis applicable to the factual findings, it should be inserted at this point in the second report.

Following the factual findings and legal analysis, the investigator should set out his or her conclusions. The investigator can reach one of three conclusions: (1) there was harassment; (2) there was no harassment; or (3) the investigation is inconclusive.

Once these conclusions are stated, the investigator should identify the employer's options for proceeding, and the recommended course of action.

4. Disclosure of the Investigation Reports

The outcome of the investigation should be communicated to the complainant and to the accused. Generally, this does not include providing copies of the final reports to the complainant, the accused, or anyone else. In fact, the report should be circulated only among the final decision-makers, as it will contain highly sensitive, personal information.

Nonetheless, there may be instances where the employer will be prepared to voluntarily release one or both reports, or where the employer will be required to disclose one or both of the reports. Where the reports are ordered by the court to be disclosed, the employer will have to comply with the court order. If the employer is a public body, the reports may have to be disclosed pursuant to a valid access to information request. Also, the reports may have to be disclosed if there is privacy legislation in force that grants employees access to their personal information.[1]

---

[1] The *Personal Information Protection and Electronic Documents Act*, S.C. 2000, c. 5, for example, applies to employees of federally-regulated businesses, works and undertakings and, except in limited circumstances, provides employees with access to all of their personal information, including this sort of investigation report. Quebec's *Act Respecting the Protection of Personal Information in the Private Sector*, R.S.Q., c. P-39.1 contains similar rights. British Columbia and Alberta currently have *Personal Information Protection Acts* in the form of draft bills before their legislatures, containing similar privacy protections and employee rights.

However, there may be times when the employer strongly objects to disclosing the investigation reports. For example, the employer may not want to disclose the second report if, for one reason or another, it did not follow the investigator's recommended course of action. Before disclosing either report, the employer should consider whether there is any legal basis for objecting to the disclosure and the implications of such objection. The employer may be able to object to disclosing one or both of the reports if the investigation was conducted by a lawyer or done in contemplation of legal action, or if the second report was written by a lawyer, in consultation with the investigator. These legal arguments are referred to as litigation privilege and solicitor-client privilege.

To preserve these potential legal arguments, it is very important that the report not be widely circulated, and that access to the report be restricted to the final decision-makers. As noted earlier in Chapter 5, sometimes employers retain a lawyer to hire the investigator, oversee the investigation and have the investigator report back to the lawyer, who in turn reports back to the employer. This is done to attempt to create an extra layer of solicitor involvement to reinforce the argument that the information is solicitor-client privileged.

◆
CHAPTER 8

DECIDING WHAT COURSE OF ACTION TO TAKE

1. Onus of Proof

The onus of proving that harassment has occurred is on the person making the complaint. The complainant must establish that harassment has occurred on a balance of probabilities. Simply defined, a balance of probabilities is 50% plus one. That is, it is more likely than not that harassment occurred. This onus of proof is not as high as in criminal cases, which require proof beyond a reasonable doubt.

2. If Harassment in the Workplace Has Occurred

If it is concluded that the complaint has merit and harassment in the workplace has occurred, the employer will have to inform the complainant and the accused that it has been determined that the conduct of the accused constituted harassment. Further, the employer will have to decide on the appropriate course of action, which includes mitigating the effects of the harassment on the complainant. There are many options for proceeding;

the following list includes the most common options, which are not mutually exclusive:

- An apology from the harasser to the complainant;
- Counselling for the harasser and other employees;
- Harassment training for the harasser and other employees;
- Disciplinary action against the accused, such as a warning, suspension or dismissal;
- Loss of a promotion or pay increase for the harasser;
- A change of duties for the complainant or the harasser;
- A transfer of work locations for the complainant or the harasser; and
- A change in the reporting relationships for the complainant or the harasser.

Deciding on the appropriate course of action is not easy. An employer should consider the nature and severity of the conduct: whether the harasser had prior training regarding workplace harassment; whether the conduct violated the employer's anti-harassment policy, if any; whether the conduct was repeated, intentional and persistent, despite the express objections of the complainant; the length of service of the accused; the prior disciplinary record of the harasser; the workplace environment; and the harasser's conduct during the investigation.

Two of these options merit special attention as they will apply in virtually every incident of harassment in the workplace: (a) education and training, and (b) disciplinary action.

2.a.   Education and Training

A key element of any response to a finding of harassment in the workplace is consideration of how a repetition of this prohibited conduct can be prevented in the future. All incidents of harassment in the workplace will warrant a review of an employer's policies and practices regarding harassment prevention and the provision of training. Very few incidents of harassment in the workplace will not require some form of workplace education, whether it is limited to the harasser or expanded broadly to the entire workplace.

An isolated incident of harassment by a rogue supervisor or a single employee that, although it may have negatively impacted a subordinate or co-worker, does not have broader workplace implications, may be addressed by requiring only the harasser to attend counselling or training courses. However, if there are multiple complainants, multiple incidents of harassment and/or multiple harassers, clearly a broader training endeavour should be undertaken.

2.b. Disciplinary Action

Given the seriousness of harassment and the clear public policy expectations that harassment will be prevented and stamped out when it occurs, employees who engage in prohibited harassment should expect significant disciplinary action as a result. This may mean dismissal, even for a single incident of misconduct.

Employers who have an anti-harassment policy in place and who have provided employees with training regarding workplace harassment will have an easier time determining the appropriate level of disciplinary action when harassment does occur. Harassers in these workplaces will have lost their ability to argue that they did not understand the proper bounds of workplace conduct.

Employers without such a policy and who have not provided anti-harassment training to employees must consider whether any of the harasser's misconduct can be reasonably excused for lack of appreciation of appropriate workplace mores. It must be noted, however that this argument has lost much of its sway in recent years. Even workplaces without an anti-harassment policy or regular training may have a corrective action plan or discipline policy. If so, the employer should apply it to situations of workplace harassment, as it would to any other situation of misconduct in the workplace.[1]

If it is determined that an employee has engaged in misconduct contrary to the anti-harassment policy, it is important that the employer should be committed to take corrective action, whatever other consequences may be implemented. Indeed, even if there is no anti-harassment policy in place, if harassment is established, then corrective action should follow. If a supervisor is not prepared to enforce adherence to the anti-harassment policy or underlying legal requirements, that supervisor is condoning the harassment, and so too is the entire management team. This is the surest route to creating a poisoned workplace.

---

[1]   J. Knight, *Managing Your Union-Free Workplace; a CLV Special Report* (Toronto: Thomson/Carswell Canada Ltd. 2002) [hereinafter Knight, *Union-Free*] at 79 to 88. See also: J. Knight, *Effective HR Management in a Union Environment; a CLV Special Report* (Toronto: Thomson/Carswell Canada Ltd., 2002) [hereinafter Knight, *Effective HR Management*] at 92 to 102.

As a general rule, discipline is supposed to be corrective in nature; it is not punitive. Employers are not meant to be the moral conscience of their employees, they are simply meant to achieve the performance that management considers to be necessary in order to achieve operational objectives. This general rule is difficult to remember in the context of a situation of harassment.

It is easy for the employer to slip into a moralistic role. This is unnecessary. The law has taken care of that. The employer is there not to be a cheerleader for the law, but to enforce it. The relevance of this point is that if there appears to be a reasonable basis for the continuation of a viable employment relationship, even when an employee has engaged in harassment misconduct, then the relationship should be continued. That is, a disciplinary consequence should be implemented that is short of dismissal. This is not a cop-out, nor is it weak. Whenever possible, the employer should prefer a measured response that preserves the employment relationship of the harasser and the complainant. Such a response is possible, of course, only where the harasser acknowledges wrongdoing and expresses a willingness to correct offensive behaviour. Also, given the seriousness of harassment, while an employee might warrant a second chance, a third chance will be rare to non-existent. The employer's obligation to provide a harassment-free workplace for its entire workforce will outweigh any obligations owed to a repeated harasser.

2.b.i.   Corrective Action Plan

The following illustrates what a corrective action plan might look like for an employee who continues to violate the anti-harassment policy. Even without an anti-harassment policy, a corrective action plan is entirely appropriate in situations of harassment that are contrary to law and common expectations.

Step 1: Written warning that expressly states that further disciplinary or corrective action, up to and including dismissal, will follow in the event of a further incident of harassment. The written warning would be accompanied by a requirement that the employee participate in whatever training or counselling measures the employer deems appropriate.

Step 2: One to three day suspension without pay, accompanied by a written warning indicating that the employee is being provided a "last chance" to continue in the workplace, and that a further incident of harassment will result in immediate dismissal. Again, the written warning may be accompanied by a requirement that the employee participate in whatever training or counselling measures the employer deems appropriate.

Step 3: Dismissal for just cause, without notice, pay in lieu of notice, or any other form of termination pay.

2.b.ii. Key Points in Considering a Corrective Action Plan

- Depending on the seriousness of the infraction, starting at Step 1 may be inappropriate; indeed, serious infractions will lead directly to a dismissal.
- Especially given the seriousness of harassment, suspensions should be without pay. It is preferable if this is stated clearly in either or both the corrective action policy and the anti-harassment policy. A unionized employee may grieve and a non-union employee may sue for wrongful dismissal, even if the consequence is an unpaid suspension and not dismissal. In either setting, an employer's defence is made much stronger if it has an anti-harassment policy and/or uses a corrective action policy and system.
- A written warning should document at least the following five points:

    (a) Briefly describe the misconduct (follow the standard tools of reporting – who, what, why, when and where);
    (b) Identify the standard or rule that was breached;
    (c) List any prior warnings;
    (d) Indicate the form of corrective action selected; and
    (e) Warn of the consequences of continuing or repeating the behaviour, that further corrective action would follow, up to and including dismissal.

- One copy of the warning goes to the employee; a second copy is retained on file. If a union is involved, depending on the language of the collective agreement, they likely would be entitled to a copy as well. Indeed, it is important to observe all formal requirements in respect of union involvement or the discipline could be invalidated.

- A suspension without pay is normally imposed for a first occurrence of a serious act of misconduct, where a decision is made that dismissal is not necessary or warranted. This may include serious forms of verbal harassment or other conduct that is clearly inappropriate. A suspension may also be imposed when an employee persists in unsatisfactory conduct or behaviour that is relatively mild in isolation, after management has attempted to have the employee correct the misconduct. As previously noted, there should be limited tolerance for multiple harassment situations. If it is not serious enough to warrant dismissal, two infractions should be sufficient for a suspension. A suspension also may be imposed where, even though there are no prior harassment situations, there is a disciplinary background that demonstrates a general pattern of misconduct.

- The dismissal of the employee will normally take place after all efforts at correcting offensive behaviour have failed. However, in some cases, the act of misconduct is of such a serious nature that management feels, from the outset, that it is left with no other option. In those cases, a dismissal for cause may issue, even though it is a first offence. Some examples include a sexual assault or a sexual solicitation or reprisal, where a supervisor is clearly abusing his or her power in respect of a subordinate employee.

- In a non-union workplace, although there is a risk that an employee could try to argue that an unpaid suspension amounts to a constructive dismissal, the only real likelihood of a legal claim is at the point of dismissal. Since management is largely unfettered in its discretion, unless there is a serious single incident that warrants immediate discharge, an employer should be patient and build the disciplinary record so long as it is reasonable to expect that the employee could be rehabilitated. The stronger the record, the easier it is to uphold a dismissal for cause at the end of the line, especially given the public policy imperative of preventing and counteracting workplace harassment.

- In a unionized workplace, there is always the potential for grievances at each stage of the corrective action process. However, the more painstaking the employer is in compiling the disciplinary record, the more likely it is that the employer will succeed in defending such grievances, including the final grievance at the point of discharge.

- It is important to ensure that disciplinary action is progressive and that harassment is not condoned in the workplace. If the message sent to employees is that management does not care about harassment, clearly the corrective action strategy adopted requires revision.

- It also is important for disciplinary action to be administered in a consistent and reasonable manner in harassment matters, as with all others. Individual decisions to correct behaviour or performance cannot be arbitrary, discriminatory, or motivated by bad faith. Given the importance of perception in applying such a system, an employer must strive to appear fair and balanced it its approach.

3. If Harassment in the Workplace Has Not Occurred or it is Inconclusive

If it is concluded that the complaint was made in good faith, but that harassment in the workplace has not occurred, or if the investigation is inconclusive, the employer will have to notify the complainant and the accused accordingly, and explain how the conclusion was reached. In addition, the employer should consider means of rehabilitating the working relationship, which may have deteriorated as a result of the complaint and investigation. This could include providing sensitivity or human rights training, to ensure the misunderstanding does not occur again. Further, it may be beneficial to reduce the extent to which the complainant and the accused work together, if possible.

If it is concluded that harassment in the workplace has not occurred and the complaint was made in bad faith, or was trivial, frivolous or vexatious, the employer will have to advise the complainant and the accused accordingly. In addition, the employer should discipline the complainant. The discipline imposed may include a written reprimand or, in extreme cases, the termination of the complainant's employment. In assessing the appropriate level of discipline to be imposed, the employer should consider the complainant's length of service and prior discipline record, the harm caused to the accused, the position of the complainant and the accused, the adverse impact on the employer, and the cost of the investigation.

◆

CHAPTER 9

LIMITING LIABILITY

In previous chapters we have provided the tools for developing and implementing an anti-harassment policy in the workplace, and for investigating a complaint of harassment should it occur. Since employers may be liable for harassment, even if they were was unaware of it, proactive prevention measures are necessary to limit liability. Proactive prevention measures not only satisfy ethical and legal obligations, they also make good, practical business sense. Fundamentally, they reduce employer liability. The policy and the investigation are the key elements of an overall strategy to minimize employer liability for workplace harassment through prevention and proper response.

The anti-harassment policy is the central communication piece to prevent complaints and to provide the framework for a proper response to any complaints of prohibited harassment. Around the policy can and should be built, the education and training pieces fundamental to ensuring that employees understand the expectations on conduct in the workplace. A policy that is used effectively will not simply exist on employee bulletin boards or in employee manuals. Rather, it will be communicated to every new employee upon hire, to every contractor on retainer, and to every existing employee through regular (typically annual) updates or refreshers. It will also be relied upon and applied consistently should any incident of harassment arise. Abiding by the commitments in the anti-harassment policy, by conducting proper investigations and imposing discipline for contraventions, is essential to an employer's credibility. Follow-through must demonstrate an employer's commitment to maintaining and promoting a positive workplace environment free from harassment.

From a liability standpoint, whether or not an employer has an anti-harassment policy in place, and how it reacts on receipt of a complaint, are key considerations for any adjudicator required to review an employer's actions, should further legal action be pursued after an internal complaint has been filed. In a case involving a complainant who was dissatisfied with her employer's response to incidents of sexual harassment by her supervisor, the tribunal identified six factors for consideration in assessing the reasonableness of the employer's response:

1. Did the employer respond promptly to the complaint?
2. Was the employer aware that sexual harassment is prohibited conduct?
3. Did the employer deal with the matter seriously?
4. Did the employer have a complaint mechanism in place?
5. Did the employer meet its obligation to provide a healthy work environment?
6. Did the employer meet its obligation to communicate its action to the complainant?[1]

If an employer receives a complaint of harassment and after an investigation it determines that harassment in the workplace occurred, the employer should take additional precautions to establish that it has done something to prevent a recurrence.

---

[1] *Wall, supra*, note 60. See also *Jones v. Amway of Canada Ltd.* (2001), 2001 C.L.L.C. 230-031 (Ont. Bd. of Inquiry), affirmed (2002), 159 O.A.C. 331 (Ont. Div. Ct.).

◆

CHAPTER 10

TAKING ACTION

This is meant as a practical book. We have tried to fill it with practical ideas to help you prevent harassment in your workplaces and to improve the effectiveness of your response in the event that harassment occurs. For human resources professionals or members of management who are intent on improving their workplaces, if you have read this book, we encourage you to take action. To assist you in formulating and executing an action plan, we suggest that each of you aspire to be a "LEADER"[1], which is a six point plan as follows:

- Leadership: Do not simply manage. Learn from yesterday. Plan for tomorrow. Act today. You are part of the directing mind of the employer. It is your legal and ethical duty to promote a positive workplace that is free from harassment. Consider the extent to which there are lessons to be learned from the employer's history and ensure that the necessary foundations are in place, such as an

---

[1] Knight, *Union-Free, supra*, note 86 at 115 to 117. See also Knight, *Effective HR Management, supra*, note 86 at 136-137.

effective policy, proper advisors, and appropriate, on-going training.

- **Excellence:** This is your workplace. You set the standards. Set those standards high. Excellence should be the goal, not just good enough. This is especially important in terms of preventing harassment in the workplace and respecting the spirit of human rights obligations, for the employer as a whole, and for every person who attends at your workplace. While we have cautioned against "zero tolerance", we certainly encourage very low tolerance for misconduct such as harassment.

- **Action:** If something happens, do something about it. Most mistakes in human resources management and in leading people happen because nothing was done when something should have been done. This is a terrible mistake if harassment occurs. We have identified appropriate responses, including a formal investigation, and several different action plans that could be suitable depending on the investigation results. Within reason, any one of those action plans is probably better than doing nothing at all.

- **Documentation:** As we have seen, there is serious liability in harassment situations, for harassers and for employers. Use formal communication systems when you have something formal to communicate, like an anti-harassment policy or discipline. Follow a standard investigation system—W7: who, to whom, what, why, when, where, and witnesses. Keep witness statements and investigation notes. Ensure thorough reports are completed.

- **Evidence:** Preserve the present. If there are items that relate to a situation (a drawing or email), then you should retain those items until the situation is fully resolved. Take photographs or videos if the place where an incident occurred is important. Alternatively and as well, use diagrams—even your own bad scratching will be much better than nothing at all. Use existing blueprints or schematics, if relevant.

- **Responsibility:** Ensure that the ultimate decision-maker has all of the information required to make the best decision. Contribute to that decision-making in a meaningful fashion.

We encourage you to use the LEADER model to help you address the issue of harassment with seriousness and dedication. We trust that you will benefit from the assistance of the concepts and practical recommendations throughout this book.

Harassment is a serious problem that requires serious attention. Beyond the liability, harassment can be very destructive to a workplace, especially if there is no effective response. As we have said throughout the book, prevent harassment if you can. However, even the best workplaces may experience harassment. If it occurs, react promptly and appropriately to stamp it out.

INDEX

threats, uttering, 47, 48

Disciplinary action *See* **Course of action, deciding**

Employer responsibility
case analyses, 23-26
    Lanteigne v. Sam' Sports Bar Ltd., 25
        employer's obligation to take action when informed of
            harassment, 25
    Mahmoodi v. University of British Columbia, 25-26
        professor creating sexualized environment with student, 26
    Simpson v. Consumers' Association of Canada, 24-25
        definition of workplace, 24-25
            whether employees perceived situations to be job related, 24
        incidents demonstrating improper conduct, 24
    Tellier v. Bank of Montreal, 23-24
conduct involving third parties, 23
conduct occurring after-hours and off-site, 22
employees vs. independent contractors, 22
far-reaching obligations of employer, 19-20
    investigation of complaints, 19
    potential respondents, 20
    scope of "employment" and "workplace", 19
organic theory of employer responsibility, 20-21
    employers' conduct relevant when remedies considered, 21
    employers jointly and severally liable with harassing employees, 21
        where employee part of "directing mind" of employer, 21
        who constituting "directing mind" of employer, 21
    liability for employees' acts in course of employment, 20-21
    Ontario Code excluding deemed liability, 21
    remedial statutes designed to "fix" situation, 20
union responsibilities, 20

Harassment in workplace
examples of harassment, 4, 8
"harassment" defined, 1
    unwelcome conduct, 1
    vexatious comment or conduct that demeans, humiliates or
        embarrasses, 1

Investigation report, how to write

disclosure of investigation reports, 79-80

    access to information request, 79

    access to report restricted, 79

    objecting to disclosure, 80

        litigation privilege and solicitor-client privilege, 80

    ordered by court, 79

    privacy legislation, 77

format of reports, 77-79

    first report: stating facts, evidence and observations, 78

    generally, 77-78

    second report: stating opinions, conclusions and recommendations, 76-77

overview, 77-78

    facts kept separate from conclusions and opinions reached, 77-78

    internal complaint, 77

    grievance under collective agreement, 77

    human rights complaint, 77

    report as evidence in external legal proceedings, 77

Investigator, selection of

background of investigator, 56

    neutrality and lack of bias, perception of, 56

    selection suiting situation, 56

importance of selecting appropriate investigator, 55-56

internal vs. external investigators, 56-60

    availability of internal, impartial, knowledgeable investigator, 58

    generally, 56-57

    identity of accused, 57-58

        senior manager necessitating external investigator, 57

        superior having ability to affect internal investigator's terms of work, whether, 57-58

        third party, allegations against, 58

        widespread allegations of harassment requiring outside investigator, 58

    legal counsel, role of, 58-59

        conducting expert investigation, 59

        coordinating or overseeing investigation, 59

        reporting back to employer, 59

harassment being illegal and wrong, xi
properly conducted investigation, ix
  increasing employee morale, ix
  leading to resolution of complaint, ix
  minimizing risks of litigation, ix
prevention of harassment in workplaces, xiii
  appropriate procedures and policies not enough, xiii
protection against unwanted discrimination and harassment, xiii

Policies *See* **Anti-harassment policies**

Remedies for harassment
civil actions, 15-17
  constructive dismissal claims by victim, 15-16
  generally, 15
  wrongful dismissal claims involving harasser, 16-17
    sexual harassment constituting just cause for termination, 16-17
    supervisors expected to provide leadership in harassment-free
workplaces, 16-17
complaints to human rights commissions, 13-15
  advocate for complainant, commission as, 13
  investigative and settlement facilitator roles, 13
  powers in respect of granting remedies, 13-14
    creative remedies, 14
    general damages, limits on awards of, 14
    mental anguish, compensation for, 14-15
      cap on damages, 14-15
    reinstatement, ability to order, 14
    restitution, power to order, 14-15
generally, 11-12
unionized employees, 12-13
  arbitration hearing informal but final and binding, 12-13
  collective agreement precluding human rights complaint, 12
  rights under human rights legislation notionally incorporated into
    agreement, 12
  violation of rights in agreement pursued through grievance and
    arbitration procedure, 11